THE CHURCH

THE CHRISTIAN STORY

A Pastoral Systematics

THE CHURCH

Signs of the Spirit
and Signs of the Times

───⊗≋⊗───

THE CHRISTIAN STORY

A Pastoral Systematics

VOLUME 5

Gabriel Fackre

WILLIAM B. EERDMANS PUBLISHING COMPANY
GRAND RAPIDS, MICHIGAN / CAMBRIDGE, U.K.

Published 2007 by

Wm. B. Eerdmans Publishing Co.

2140 Oak Industrial Drive N.E., Grand Rapids, Michigan 49505 /
P.O. Box 163, Cambridge CB3 9PU U.K.

Printed in the United States of America

12 11 10 09 08 07   7 6 5 4 3 2 1

Library of Congress Cataloging-in-Publication Data

Fackre, Gabriel J.

The church: signs of the spirit and signs of the times / Gabriel Fackre.

p.   cm.

ISBN 978-0-8028-3392-1 (pbk.: alk. paper)

1. Church.   2. Holy Spirit.   I. Title.

BV600.3.F33 2007

262 — dc22

2006029021

www.eerdmans.com

To Dorothy

life partner in ministry and mission

Contents

Introduction

*U*nder the Steeple was a long-ago first attempt at ecclesiology by the writer and spouse.[1] Inspiration for it came from attending the 1954 assembly of the World Council of Churches in Evanston, Illinois. We were struck by the parallels between the variety of perspectives found in that dramatic event in conciliar Christianity and the diversity of what we called in that book the "clans" in the congregation.[2] The ecumenical movement's quest for unity amidst diversity under the Lordship of Christ seemed to be the same as the one we faced in our mill town charge in the steel valley of Pittsburgh. Indeed, the players were similar. Those in our congregations who viewed church, first and foremost, as worship, or preaching, or fellowship, or action (with the rooms in a church building reflecting these accents) had their counterparts in traditions and denominations that featured one or another practice. Avery Dulles, decades later, explored a like ecclesial diversity in terms of "models of the church." The same types re-

---

1. Gabriel and Dorothy Fackre, *Under the Steeple* (Nashville: Abingdon Press, 1957). We used the child's finger poem as the framework: "This is the church, this is the steeple, open the doors, see all the people."

2. Church sociologist Victor Obenhaus told us that his studies of congregations discovered, through social scientific methods, what we discerned intuitively. His data and conclusions are recorded in Victor Obenhaus, *See the People: A Study of the United Church of Christ* (Chicago: Chicago Theological Seminary, 1968).

appeared in that taxonomy as "sacrament," "herald," "mystical communion," and "servant."[3]

Now, a half-century after *Under the Steeple*, the question arises for this pastoral systematics: What, if any, is the relation there found, and still to be found, at St. John's-by-the-Gas-Station, and also in the wider Christian community, to the topics usually dealt with in a doctrine of the church? The creedal attributes of the church — unity, sanctity, catholicity, apostolicity? The marks of the church in the Reformation tradition — the pure preaching of the Word and the right administration of the sacraments? The signs of the Holy Spirit at the church's Pentecostal birth described in the early chapters of Acts? The New Testament images of the church with their trinitarian import as "the body of Christ," the "temple of the Spirit," "the people of God"? The church as a divine-human institution?

A case will be made in this work for a relationship between the empirical reality in which the pastor lives and works and the ecclesial Reality described in doctrinal terms. In fact, there is a striking analogy between the classical attributes and marks and the varied accents found in both congregational and supra-congregational life. Parallels to (and the origins of?) these attributes and marks had their first expression in the *charisms* emerging at the birth of the church, so delineated in the report of the event (Acts 2–4).[4] That story was the launching point in Volume 1 of this series for treating the doctrine of the church. Here too the New Testament

---

3. Avery Dulles, *Models of the Church: A Critical Assessment of the Church in All Its Aspects* (Garden City, N.Y.: Doubleday, 1974). Added to the four cited was a fifth, "institution." I have argued elsewhere that this was an apple among the oranges, signifying more the routinizing of one or another of the four charisms. Gabriel Fackre, *The Christian Story*, vol. 1, *A Narrative Interpretation of Basic Christian Doctrine*, 3rd edition (Grand Rapids: Eerdmans, 1996), p. 159.

4. Of course, there are anticipations of the same in the community of disciples before Pentecost grounded in the diverse ministry of Jesus, before that in the Old Testament gathering of a people of God, and after that in the heavenly church triumphant. However wider and longer the nature of the church can be stretched, the pentecostal birth of the Body of Christ on earth is our present focus and the reality/Reality in which pastors find themselves. Other volumes in this series will take up the relation of the Jewish people and the eschatological church triumphant to this church in its givens. For the direction in which such will be developed regarding the Jewish people, see Gabriel Fackre, "The Covenant with Israel: Elective Action" in *The Doctrine of Revelation: A Narrative Interpretation*, Edinburgh Studies in Constructive Theology (Edinburgh: Edinburgh University Press, 1997 and Grand Rapids: Eerdmans, 1997), pp. 105-19.

account of those "signs of the Spirit"[5] will be foundational, along with their ecumenical identification as *kerygma, leitourgia, diakonia,* and *koinonia.*[6] The interpretation of the foursomes and twosome and their interrelationships will take unconventional tacks at times, as soon will become apparent.

Another New Testament resource for explicating the doctrine of the church is its variety of "images," given currency by the influential typology of Paul Minear in his *Images of the Church in the New Testament.* They will also provide biblical touchstones for interpreting another aspect of the doctrine: its relation to the triune God and the church as a divine-human institution. The doctrine of the Trinity and its relation to ecclesiology in other respects will also be taken up.

With a charismatic gift goes a demand. The questions addressed to both the church local and the church at large a half-century ago in *Under the Steeple* and at Evanston had to do with the faithful stewardship of the *charisms.* How are the gifts of Christ opened, and then shared? The answer to these questions, then and since, can shed light on what the ecclesiological indicatives and imperatives mean for us today.

Much commented upon is Karl Barth's significant change from writing a "Christian dogmatics" to launching his great project of a "*church* dogmatics." The lesson needs to be learned ever and again. The "constructive theology" of the twenty-first century too often is the construct of individual theologians as they reflect on traditional or new themes in abstraction from the living reality of the church. Systematic theology, as here understood, is theology-in-the-round, engaging all the classical loci, but doing it from deep within the life of the church, and as a service to the preaching and teaching of the church.[7] As a "pastoral systematics," this treatment of the doctrine of the church will give much attention to the day-to-day setting of the pastor's work and witness. Ecclesiology written to aid pastors in

5. "Signs of the Spirit" is often associated with movements of "enthusiasm" in church history, as for example in Howard A. Snyder, *Signs of the Spirit* (Grand Rapids: Zondervan, 1989). Here we follow rather the ecumenical usage cited.

6. See, for example, their use in J. C. Hoekendijk, *Horizons of Hope* (Nashville: Tidings, 1970).

7. For helpful comments on "the understanding of the task of Christian theology in its ecclesial setting," especially as contrasted to "a good deal of contemporary dogmatic and systematic theology," see John Webster, *Holiness* (Grand Rapids: Eerdmans, 2003), p. 4 and "Introduction," pp. 1-7.

their ministry must show the relationship of sound doctrine to real life. Volume 2 in this series began with an autobiographical account of an effort in one ecclesial setting to retrieve classical Christian teaching.[8] This volume also will give significant space to ecclesial as well as biblical narrative, drawing on the writer's involvement in the church struggle over half a century as a pastor, a teacher of pastors, and parishioner. In Chapter 2 with its "ecclesial narrative" the writer's own denomination, of necessity, will be given attention. However, that communion, the United Church of Christ, has in its twentieth-century history been a bellwether in mainline Protestantism regarding response to cultural trends and thus is a laboratory of learning for those in many other traditions.

Attention to the day-to-day life of the church will be given at two levels, the church local and the church at large. This doctrine is a particularly apt locus for the confluence of the pastoral and the narrational, dealing as it does with the tangibilities of faith, claims made for what goes on in the building to which the reader regularly treks, and among the people in it and beyond it with their common practices. Systematic ecclesiologies, of course, deal with profound intangibles, and to those we shall attend throughout. Yet here an attempt will be made to relate our inquiry into the meaning of the church to the empirical realities.[9] To adapt a fine phrase of Dietrich Bonhoeffer to this topic, as Christ is "haveable" in the seeable, touchable, and tastable givens, so too is the mystical Body of Christ.[10] William Willimon makes this point in his account of the first year of his ministry as a Methodist bishop:

---

8. So the initial Craigville Colloquies that have continued as annual events to this day. See *The Christian Story*, vol. 2, *Authority: Scripture in the Church for the World* (Grand Rapids: Eerdmans, 1987), pp. 3-41.

9. While this close attention to personally and ecclesially experienced historical realities is a mark of this series and particularly its ecclesiology, this work is done against the background of standard systematics works, the recent surge in which has been of special interest to the writer. So his surveys: "Reorientation and Retrieval in Seminary Theology," *The Christian Century* 108, no. 20 (June 26-July 3, 1991): 82-83; "The Revival of Systematic Theology," *Interpretation* 49, no. 3 (July 1995): 229-41; "The Surge in Systematics: A Commentary on Current Works," *Journal of Religion* 73, no. 2 (April 1993): 223-27; and "In Quest of the Comprehensive: The Systematics Revival," *Religious Studies Review* 20, no. 1 (January 1994): 7-12.

10. Indeed, that is what Bonhoeffer meant: Christ is "'haveable,' graspable in his Word within the Church." See *Act and Being*, trans. Bernard Noble, Introduction by Ernst Wolf (New York: Harper & Bros, 1961), p. 91.

The good news is that most of what bishops do is mundane. . . . More good news is that most of what the Trinity does is mundane too. And local. After all the Word was made flesh in Bethlehem before it went to Washington, London or Paris. The great genius of Protestant Christianity is in the living, breathing local communities of faith, congregations that struggle to embody that which they profess in places only Jesus could love. God is forcing me to take the side roads and attend to the local and the particular, to eat copious barbeque and to lie awake at night worrying about the kingdom of God in Alabaster, Alabama.[11]

The importance of theology for pastors, and for theologians, to take account of the realities of pastoral ministry in their own work — the premise of this series — is underscored by two developments in contemporary North American church life. In addition to the serious theological problems in the current state of the mainline churches to be chronicled in Chapter 2, there are significant opportunities for the partnership of *theologia* and *pastoralia* in these newer phenomena. One of them is the "purpose-driven church" movement centered in the ministry of Rick Warren,[12] and the other is the increasing trend for congregations in mainline churches (especially ethnic and rural congregations), as well as in non-denominational evangelical congregations large and small, to be served by pastors without conventional seminary preparation.

The Rick Warren phenomenon — both the Saddleback congregation of twenty thousand members and its modeling for, and outreach to, thousands of pastors in North America and overseas — cannot be ignored by mainline churches dismissive of megachurch deviation from standard practice. Perhaps it takes secular attention, as that of a perceptive *New Yorker* article,[13] to make us aware that this is the Protestant counterpart of "Jesuit" marching orders, the training of a virtual order of pastors in many countries related through the Internet and simulcast television as well as

11. William H. Willimon, "Dispatch from Birmingham: First-Year Bishop," *The Christian Century* 122, no. 19 (September 20, 2005): 28.

12. Rick Warren, *The Purpose-Driven Church: Growth Without Compromising Your Message and Mission* (Grand Rapids: Zondervan, 1995) and *The Purpose-Driven Life: What on Earth Am I Here For?* (Grand Rapids: Zondervan, 2002).

13. Malcolm Gladwell, "The Cellular Church," *The New Yorker* (September 19, 2005), pp. 60-67.

standard publishing methods to the Saddleback concepts of ministry and their effect not only on church growth but on service to human need, such that the "signs of the Spirit" to be discussed throughout this volume are discernible.

The purpose-driven phenomenon has shown the importance of ministry to pastors and in turn their crucial catalytic role in the life and mission of congregations. In characteristically exuberant overstatement but not without its kernel of truth, Warren declares, against the background of a campaign to address the AIDS crisis in Africa,

> There is only one thing big enough to handle the world's problems, and that is millions and millions of churches spread around the world. . . . I can take you to thousands of villages where they don't have a school. They don't have a grocery store, don't have a fire department. But they do have a church. They do have a pastor. . . .[14]

Yet, as acknowledged by its leadership, as well as can be seen from the content of its publications and sermons in circulation, the need for theological depth and acquaintance with the classical Christian tradition is manifest.[15] Regarding the doctrine of the church here explored, how important for pastors and congregations given gifts of the Holy Spirit to understand what the Great Tradition has learned in its long history of the stewardship of these graces and how they are related to one another. How important, as well, for that network of evangelical pastors and congregations to make connection with the church ecumenical so that on critical theological matters there can take place the mutual affirmation and admonition so necessary for the Body's health (1 Cor. 12).[16]

The second phenomenon is the growth of a "second track" of prepara-

14. Gladwell, "The Cellular Church," p. 67.

15. For a critique from within evangelical ranks, see Jonathan R. Wilson, "Whose Purpose, Whose Drive? Thinking Teleologically About Purpose-Drivenness," *Reformation and Revival Journal* 14, no. 2 (2005): 55-65.

16. An example of an admonishment directed at the temptations of the "contemporary" comes from Willimon, who despairing of theological and liturgical "fog" in his own backyard where he "can't tell the difference between aging 'liberals' and bogus 'evangelicals,' between Shelby Spong and Rick Warren," arguing that we can't do battle with today's evils in and outside the churches "if we have weapons that are merely contemporary, purpose-driven techniques or heart-happy liberal accommodations. We need theological refurbishment" ("Dispatch from Birmingham: First-Year Bishop," p. 29).

tion for ordained ministry given growing accreditation in the mainline churches, and needed as well by pastors of independent congregations or ethnic and evangelical communions that serve without the traditional four years of college and three years of seminary training. While on-the-ground experience and non-traditional or self-taught preparation may, indeed, have equivalencies to, and in some cases superior faithfulness in content and commitment to, the current academy's disciplines, they are no substitutes for immersion in the 2000-year lore of the church universal, and "the love of God with the mind" represented by careful biblical and theological learning. To think "systematically" — that is to say, coherently — about who God is, who we are, what the church is, and where the world is headed according to the Grand Narrative can only enrich the week-to-week preaching and day-to-day teaching that must go on in any congregation seeking to be faithful to the gospel in this second growing grassroots world of the church, even as those of us in oldline denominations of presumed "learned ministry," in turn, learn from these brothers and sisters.

Because the day-to-day life of congregations and the work of systematic theology are in necessary partnership, we make no apologies here for the personal narrative of the former taken up in Chapter 2. For all that, pride of normative place will be given to the biblical story out of which the doctrine of the church rises, and hence the importance of the account of the church's birth and the New Testament images of the church. Therefore we get our bearings, initially, from the *ekklesia* as Scripture tells of its being and doing.

PART I

SEEING THE SIGNS

CHAPTER 1

Discerning the Signs of the Spirit

The Church in Acts

The New Testament story of Pentecost reports on the birthmarks of the Body of Christ. In continuity with the treatment of the doctrine in Volume 1, we draw on its description of the appearance of these stigmata with indications of the fuller exposition to come. In the earlier volume the link was made from the first chapter in the book of Acts with its the ascent of the Son/sun of God to the heavens to the second chapter's report of the descent therefrom of the rays of divine light, their power leaving "signs of the Spirit," and thence outward from birth and nurture into mission in the third and fourth chapters.

Kerygma

The Holy Spirit fires the people of God to say what it sees. The first act of the empowered people is *kerygma*, the report of the good news, the proclamation of the gospel. Thus Peter called onlookers to "listen to what I have to say [about] Jesus of Nazareth, a man attested to you by God with deeds of power . . ." (Acts 2:22). So the Christian story is told. And it is told against the background and in the idiom of the people of the Covenant, out of whose history this new Word comes. Peter presses the narrative back into the Prologue, "the definite plan and foreknowledge of God . . ." (Acts 2:23), and forward from that to crucifixion, resurrection, and ascension, and thence to the call to those who heard this Word to join the unfolding drama. As the message has an audience in mind, it is addressed here to the "house of Israel." The narration of the Tale of the deeds of God, the *telling* of the Story, is a sign of the presence of the Spirit, and a tool the Spirit uses to build the church. The *kerygma,* therefore, is a constitutive factor of the Christian community. Where the Word is preached, the Body of Christ takes form in the world.

Leitourgia

The stirrings of the Spirit continue.

> So those who welcomed his message were baptized, and that day about three thousand persons were added. They devoted themselves to the apostles' teaching and fellowship, to the breaking of bread and the prayers. . . . Day by day, as they spent much time together in the temple, they broke bread at home and ate their food with glad and generous hearts, praising God. . . . (Acts 2:41-42, 46-47)

Prayer and praise, the waters of baptism and the bread of the supper, these gifts of the Spirit and worship acts of the people appear in the midst of the aborning congregation. *Leitourgia* joins *kerygma* as a sign of the Spirit. The church *celebrates* as well as tells the Story. In the sacramental form of baptism and eucharist an "outward and visible sign" of the Spirit complements the verbal one of proclamation. Word and sacrament keep company in sustaining the life of the church. Yet the sacramental signs do not exhaust the liturgical life of the Body. Corporate prayer and praise in their multifarious expressions, meditative and celebrative, are vehicles of the Spirit in maintaining and strengthening the Body of Christ. The prayers and songs of the church keep the people of God in communion with the purposes of God. In worship the Spirit keeps the Body moving by the eye of faithful prayer and praise turned toward the Horizon.

The life of prayer is at the center of worship, communal or personal. Prayer, mental or verbal, is conscious communication with God. Here an I

4

meets a Thou, the human person encounters the divine Self. Prayer in Christian idiom is offered "through Jesus Christ our Lord." Christ is the reference point for our supplication and adoration.

In the acts of prayer, praise, confession, thanksgiving, intercession, petition, and commitment we are catapulted forward to meet the coming Lord. Prayer therefore frees us from bondage to the present moment, gives perspective on it and leverage in dealing with it. But it is not these pragmatic benefits of "spirituality" that justify prayer. In fact they can only be had when they are not sought. ". . . strive first for the kingdom of God and his righteousness, and all these things will be given to you as well" (Matt. 6:33). It is the love of God for God's own sake, the company kept with the One who comes, that is the ultimate warrant for what we do on our knees before our Maker and Redeemer.

Diakonia

> All who believed were together and had all things in common; they would sell their possessions and goods and distribute the proceeds to all, as any had need. (Acts 2:44-45)

As the Spirit opens the eye of faith to see the Light, so it empowers the visionary community as well to see *in* the Light the brother and sister in Christ. Illumination by the divine Light means in this instance *diakonia,* a serving of the neighbor in need within the Christian community. This meant a very radical act of physical support in the primitive church, pooling of property and possessions and redistribution on the principle "to each according to need." As this commitment worked itself out in the ensuing life of the community, it took the form of care for, and the honoring of the dignity of, the dysfunctional within ancient society, the "nobodies" of that culture: widow, orphan, prisoner, slave, poor. The church demonstrated the meaning of *agape* in its internal life, *doing* the Story, loving the unloved, and thus intuitively modeling the quality of life in the Realm to come. Servanthood comes naturally to be a gift of the Spirit of a shalom in which the bondages of deprivation and indignity are challenged, and the broken *bodies* of human beings are made whole by bread and wine and water as well as broken *spirits* are healed.

How diakonia is enacted is related to each situation of need. The form of servanthood may be the communitarian caring of the earliest Christians or the mercy and justice ministries of later ones. And its neighbor may be the slave and orphan of the first century or the aged and marginalized of the present. *Diakonia* continues in each new setting to be a sign of the Spirit in the church, a matter to be subsequently explored.

Koinonia

> They met constantly . . . to share the common life. . . . With one mind they kept up their daily attendance at the temple, and, breaking bread in private houses, shared their meals with unaffected joy. . . . (Acts 2:42, 46)

Sharing the common life and meals was more than a ministry of material benevolence. In and through the *diakonia* was the throb of *koinonia*. The Spirit gives the gift of *being* as well as doing: being together. *Koinonia* is the life together of sister and brother in Christ, *being* the Story. Luther spoke of it as the "mutual conversation and consolation" of the brothers and sisters. Here joys are shared and burdens are borne. The somewhat tepid word "fellowship" points to, but does not adequately convey community as it is relived by the people of God wherever the Holy Spirit is at work. *Koinonia* happens when there is an authentic "common life," a sharing and caring "life together" (Bonhoeffer) in which the people of God dwell in the joyful unity of the Spirit.

Signs Pointing Out

When the Holy Spirit descended on the first Christians its fires drove them out into the world. Acts 3 and 4 tell that story.

> One day Peter and John were going up to the temple at the hour of prayer. . . . And a man lame from birth was being carried in. People would lay him daily at the gate of the temple called the Beautiful Gate so he could ask for alms from those entering the temple. . . . Peter looked intently at him, as did John, and said, "Look at us. . . . I have no silver and gold, but what I have I give you; in the name of Jesus Christ of Nazareth, stand up and walk." (Acts 3:1-6)

On the very heels of this deed of mercy comes a word:

> "... why do you wonder at this...? The God of Abraham, the God of Isaac, the God of Jacob, the God of our ancestors has glorified Jesus...." (Acts 3:12, 13)

Whereupon, Peter for the second time in this account of Christian beginnings tells the story of God as it pertained to this people — its prophets and its hopes, its blessing by Jesus' coming, his suffering, death, and resurrection, its bringing of the "universal restoration."

Taken together, two of the signs of the Spirit have now pointed outward. If Acts 2 is about the *nurture* of the church as a gathering of telling, celebrating, doing, and being, then Acts 3 and Acts 4 are about the *mission* of the church. Pentecost is also about an outward-bound people. *Missio* is sending, a sending integral to the being of what and who one is, even as the missions of the triune God are about Persons who, as such, of course, are more than their Work — the eternal Father creating, the eternal Son reconciling, the eternal Spirit redeeming. Emil Brunner had it almost, but not quite, right in his much-quoted words: "The church exists by mission as fire by burning." The church exists by the pentecostal fires of the Spirit, but they become what they already are in the sweep of mission.

A close reading of the two chapters on mission will find the other two signs of the Spirit outward bound. *Leitourgia* joins *diakonia* and *kerygma* in the praise sent heavenward for all outside to see:

> All the people saw him walking and praising God ... [before the "rulers of the people"] all of them praised God for what had happened. ... After they were released, they went to their friends. ... When they heard it, they raised their voices together. ... (Acts 3:8; 4:21, 23, 24)

The prayerful praises of the church are sent on their way into the public square as witness to the people and structures of power. The same is true for *koinonia*. It was visible to those outside as well as inside:

> Now the whole group of those who believed were of one heart and soul. ... (Acts 4:32)

Again, remarked upon as evidence of that life together was the fact that no one claimed private ownership of any possessions, but everything they owned was held in common. (Acts 4:32)

How could this public visibility of radical *koinonia* not have prompted the comment attributed to outsiders, "See how those Christians love one another"?

Mission is the God-given outreach of the church that rises from a God-given inreach. The consequences of mission are lessons for us to learn. On the one hand,

. . . many of those who heard the word believed; and they numbered about five thousand. (Acts 4:4)

Seeds planted in fertile soil spring up. On the other hand, there are the rocks and brambles. The power brokers of the day were "much annoyed":

So they arrested them and put them in custody. . . . (Acts 4:3)

Mission brings trouble as well as triumph, mission of word and also deed, for imprisonment had to do with *diakonia* as well as *kerygma:*

A good deed done to someone who was sick. . . . (Acts 4:9)

From this account of our founding forebears we are left with much to ponder. Such is the burden of the chapters to follow. How much of this can be replicated today? Miraculous healing? Holding all things in common? Arrest? To be continued.

What happened at Pentecost? The Body of Christ was born on earth, formed by and filled with the Holy Spirit, and living under the known sovereignty of its exalted Lord. The Spirit keeps the Body alive and alert, empowering a people to tell and celebrate, to do and be the Story — *kerygma, leitourgia, diakonia, koinonia.* "Come Holy Spirit!"

To What End?

The question is twofold. What is the conclusion of the church, its *finis?* What is the purpose of the church, its *telos?*

Finis

The final chapter of the Christian Story is the consummation of all things. In this new heaven and new earth there will be the life together that God is and wills for creation. In the kingdom that Christ promised there will be no hate or hurt, the swords of nations beaten into plowshares in a holy commonwealth and sanctity in the heart of every inhabitant. And joy as well in everlasting praise to the Maker and Redeemer. What we know in part about the being and doing of God will then be known in full.

Do these qualities of the kingdom come sound familiar? They are the fullness of the gifts of *koinonia, diakonia, leitourgia, and kerygma* given to the church in the time before the End. Thus the ecclesial work of the Holy Spirit pours out charisms with the foretaste of Things to Come, signs and portents of the End. We are given a glimpse of what is to be as the winds of the Spirit blow through the church, and the fires of the Spirit descend upon it.

Stated otherwise, we enter at Pentecost into the third act of the creedal drama, the mission of the Holy Spirit within the whole trinitarian *Missio Dei*, the encompassing "mission of God."

> I believe in the Holy Spirit, the holy catholic church, the communion
> of saints, the forgiveness of sins, the resurrection of the body and the
> life everlasting. (Apostles' Creed)

That mission brings to be the church on earth and the communion of saints in heaven by the forgiveness of sins, all pointing toward the Holy Spirit's work in the finale of this act in the resurrection of the dead and the life everlasting. As the one mission of the Spirit, there is continuity between the birth of the holy catholic church and the consummation of all things in the life everlasting. Thus in that Finale *no church* as we know it is to be found.

> I saw no temple in the city. . . . (Rev. 21:22)

The reason is the universal spread of the signs of the Spirit in the life everlasting when God is "all, and in all."

> For its temple is the Lord God Almighty and the Lamb. (Rev. 21:22)

While each of the three missions brings one of the three Persons of the Trinity to the fore, the unity of the triune God is such that all participate in

9

every work in the divine economy; the Spirit is the Spirit of the Son of the Father.

The church's eucharist is of special significance in this linkage of *ekklesia* to *eschaton*. We shall explore its meaning in more detail in Chapter 5. Here the judgment of the ecumenical convergence document, *Baptism, Eucharist and Ministry*, is pertinent, as it describes one aspect of the eucharist as a "meal of the Kingdom":

> The Holy Spirit through the eucharist gives a foretaste of the king-dom of God; the church receives the life of the new creation and the assurance of the Lord's return. . . . The eucharist opens up the vision of the divine rule which has been promised as the final renewal of creation, and as a foretaste of it . . . the world which is promised is present in the whole eucharistic celebration. The world is present in the thanksgiving to the Father, where the Church speaks on behalf of the whole creation; in the memorial of Christ, where the Church, united with its great High Priest and Intercessor, prays for the world; in the prayer for the gift of the Holy Spirit, where the Church asks for sanctification and new creation.[1]

Thus both in the church's ecclesial circumference and at its eucharistic center, the signs of the Spirit are signs of the coming kingdom, the con-summation of the divine purposes.

As the vision of the anticipated End discloses, what the Holy Spirit gives to the church is what God wills for the world. Eschatology, the chap-ter in the story about the ultimate gift of God, becomes, therefore, the pen-ultimate mandate in the chapter on ecclesiology. The church lives with the commission to witness in the world to what it has been given in its own life. Thus the mission (*missio,* sending) of the Spirit to the church becomes the mission, the sending, of the church. All the signs of the Spirit are pointed outward from their presence inward; inreach has its partner in outreach. These aspects will be explored throughout, and a chart of their interrelationship appears in the Conclusion.

1. World Council of Churches, Faith and Order Commission, *Baptism, Eucharist and Ministry,* Faith and Order Paper No. 111 (Geneva: World Council of Churches, 1982), pp. 13, 14.

Telos

Implicit in all the foregoing is a scandalous claim. Not only does the church witness to the world through the signs of the Spirit what will be at the End, but it also *participates* now, albeit brokenly, in the kingdom that is to come. Those who trust the *kerygma,* truly celebrate that gospel in the *leitourgia,* and live out that faith in the love poured forth in *diakonia* and *koinonia,* are citizens of the Realm to be.

In some interpretations of the purpose of the church, its reason for being is construed solely in terms of disclosure. It is given the Story and is called to witness to it in all it says, does, and is.

> The Church lives in order that the world may know its true being. It is *pars pro toto;* it is the firstfruits of the new creation.[2]

In such an ecclesiology, revelation is to the fore, indeed a high view of it. The church is granted a singular Word which it is called to share with the world.[3] Yet the church is a "realm of redemption"[4] as well as a realm of revelation. The Holy Spirit's signs give what they point to, participation now in the reconciliation which is to be. Thus the purpose of the church is both to gather a community that witnesses to the drama of redemption and also a community that shares in that very life with God. Life with God is life with the triune God. The Holy Spirit, as the Spirit of the Son, joins those given the signs to all the Persons of the Trinity. Life in the church of *kerygma, leitourgia, diakonia,* and *koinonia* is union with Christ and through him with the Father by the power of the Spirit. These are matters of redemption, justification, sanctification, and regeneration yet to be dealt with in a subsequent volume on soteriology, but to be presumed in any treatment of ecclesiology.[5]

---

2. "Preliminary Remarks," *The Church for Others: Two Reports on the Missionary Structure of the Congregation* (Geneva: World Council of Churches, 1967), p. 18.

3. The influence of Karl Barth was a factor in *The Church for Others* project to be later discussed, the writer a participant.

4. The name of a volume on ecclesiology by Robert Nelson.

5. Treated in a preliminary way in *The Christian Story,* vol. 1, *A Narrative Interpretation of Basic Christian Doctrine,* 3rd edition (Grand Rapids: Eerdmans, 1996), pp. 188-209. Taken up also in Gabriel Fackre, Ronald H. Nash, and John Sanders, *What About Those Who Have Never Heard?* (Downers Grove, Ill.: InterVarsity Press, 1995), pp. 71-95 and *passim.*

The doctrine of the Trinity bears on the doctrine of the church in other ways as well. We turn to them.

The Signs of the Spirit of the Triune God

Miroslav Volf in an important work, *After Our Likeness: The Church as the Image of the Trinity*, explores the ecclesiological implications of various views of the Trinity (notably that of Joseph Ratzinger and John Zizioulas), constructing his own in a "Free Church" tradition that learns from but also critiques the hierarchical ecclesiologies of the Roman Catholic and Eastern Orthodox traditions of Ratzinger and Zizioulas, related as they are to "monistic" and "monarchical" tendencies in their understanding of the relation of the Persons to one another.[6] As we have brought to the fore here the Person and Work of the Holy Spirit as key to the doctrine of the church, what is the relation of the Trinity as a whole to the nature of the church?

Volf makes a case for an ecclesiology that is grounded in the mutualities of the Persons, one that does not depend on an ecclesial substance over and beyond the local church (a "whole church" on which the congregation depends for its existence, signaled especially by an episcopacy or papacy). Yet he finds a place for the ecumenical impulse which presses the congregation to covenantal relations with that larger community, drawing on the wisdom of its lore as well as making its own contribution to it. Is there another way to read the relationship of the local to the universal that acknowledges the veracity of Volf's concerns? We shall take up the specific issue of episcopal ministry when dealing with the church's attribute of apostolicity, but here the broader question is the relation of the one to the many — the church universal to the "assembly of believers" — as in the Acts congregation described as paradigmatic for the being of the church.

God is a Mutuality in which the Persons, each with a singular relational identity, so inhere in one another that the "They" become a Thou. God *is* Love. This divine "Life Together" has its ecclesial counterpart, in broken human analogy, in the life together of the church. So the Spirit's sign of

---

6. Miroslav Volf, *After Our Likeness: The Church as the Image of the Trinity* (Grand Rapids: Eerdmans, 1998).

koinonia given to the New Testament congregation. Yet we have seen four signs, all of the Spirit, and therefore, reflecting in their inseparability the same mutuality that marks the Life Together of the triune God. As the New Testament assembly comes to be church by the grace of these signs, so any like assembly in any time and place with their gifts constitutes "church." This is the valid point made by Volf, arrived at here by the route of discerning the New Testament signs of the Spirit.

However, we live now and not then. How do congregations emerge today, and how have they come into existence since New Testament times? Certainly not out of the "thin air." Christianity is a historical religion, of a piece with the trajectory of Israel, centered in an incarnate event, and continued in an empirical community viewing itself as the very Body of Christ on earth. The heirs of the New Testament church continued in many and diverse ways, dramatically divided in 1054, split again in the Reformation era, continued these fissiparous tendencies ever and again, and to this day produce ever-new gatherings that explode into being in pentecostal fever or are organized by charismatic self-designated preachers or inspired lay leadership, and on and on.

When and where these expressions of Christian life together show the signs of the Spirit of Acts 2–4, they have come from some previous ecclesial stream where they learned their *kerygma, leitourgia, diakonia, koinonia,* even if only to disagree with and dissociate themselves from this ancestry and its interpretation of the Book, the teaching, the worship, the doing and being of their forebears.

While the local church that displays the signs of the Spirit may think itself independent from the church as a whole, it does, empirically, rely on that larger church's prior existence. Theologically considered, the life that it is granted by the Holy Spirit, is the Spirit of the Son who has been among us on earth in his Body of Christ since its pentecostal birth. While contesting, often rightly so, the particular shape that Body has taken, given its human underside, it is inseparable from that historic lineage. And why would that not be so, given the trinitarian Life Together out of which the church comes? "Life together," not "life apart," in time — diachronically — is a natural expression of the Love that God is. Local churches, whether they acknowledge it or not, are bound together in fact and before God. As Rowan Williams astutely observed in another connection regarding the bonding of all Christians by a common past in "association with Christ," Christians thus participate in one network of relations, organized around the pivotal relation with Jesus and his relation with God into which Christians are inducted.[7]

Indeed, as the Mercersburg theologians John Nevin and Philip Schaff argued, the very Life of God comes in the incarnate Christ and passes to us in our union with Christ in the church and its central event the eucharist. We shall return to these themes.

As there is such a life together in time, why not also in space? Here the imperative joins the indicative. The ecumenical imperative declares: be what you are! You are, before God and in history, the one Body of Christ. Therefore, fulfill your purpose by bringing your charism to others and by receiving that of others in the one Body. Once again unity-in-Deity and diversity-in-Persons enters as the source of the church's mutualities.

The Mission of God and the Story of God

During the decade of the 1960s (which we shall examine in our Chapter 2 review of twentieth-century ecclesiology), the concept of *missio Dei,* the mission of God, came to the fore in theological circles concerned to relate the church to the social ethical challenges of the time, especially race, peace, and poverty.[8] This view sought to show how the church's mission was inextricable from God's overall mission in the world as that of bringing about *shalom,*

> a social happening, an event in interpersonal situations [in which] each time a man is a true neighbor, each time men live for others, the life giving action of God is to be discerned.[9]

This view entailed a relationship of God to the world that differed from what was seen to be the conventional one. The sequence in the relationship

7. Rowan Williams, *Why Study the Past? The Quest for the Historical Church* (Grand Rapids: Eerdmans, 2005), p. 29.

8. The report of the World Council of Churches' West European and North American "Working Groups on the Missionary Structure of the Congregation" was an influential document in the emergence of this concept as in the combined report cited earlier, technically identified as *The Church for Others and The Church for the World* (Geneva: World Council of Churches, 1968). The writer was a member of the North American Working Group.

9. *The Church for Others*, pp. 14, 15.

was not God–church–world, but God–world–church. The church existed authentically only when it was engaged in the social happening of *shalom,* thus putting it in touch with the true work of God in the world. In practice this meant, in the extreme, that the church existed only as secular movements engaged with the critical social issues of the day, the local congregation being deemed obsolete — preoccupied as it was with "churchy" matters rather than the goal of "humanization." In other expressions, the *missio Dei* proponents sought to challenge "morphological fundamentalism" by creating "new forms" of church life that were seen to be the true agents of *shalom,* such as industrial missions, urban training centers, coffee houses, national church-sponsored civil rights actions, etc.[10] We shall return to the discussion of this accent on *diakonia* in Chapter 2. Here we attend to the doctrinal underpinning of *missio Dei.*

The "mission of God" as that is understood in this work is the mission of the triune God. As such, it entails three missions: the mission of the Father in creation, the mission of the Son in reconciliation, the mission of the Spirit in sanctification. All of these "doings" of the triune God are rooted in the divine "being." The being of God, the immanent Trinity, is a Life Together in perfect unity of the three divine Persons finding expression in the doing of the economic Trinity. Who God is is what God wills, and thus the purpose of a life together for whatever God brings to be. Translated into the terms of the *missio Dei* movement: God is *Shalom* and God thus wills *shalom.*

In the biblical account, God brings into being a world and wills for it a life together — with God and with all creation. This is chapter 1 in the Christian Story, the mission of God to create *shalom.* However, there is a second chapter — the stumble and fall of the world away from the divine invitation. Sin resists *shalom.* More is needed to bring it to be, and thus the Story goes forward, as in the grace of preservation in the covenant with Noah and in the election of Israel with the promises entailed, that the Creator will not give up on the world as God's covenant partner. To deal with sin, evil, and death that have resisted the divine purpose, a radical act is needed, a second mission of the triune God, a veritable entry of Deity into the fallen world, there to contest in its own form and on its own ground the powers that militate against God's will for the world. So comes the mission of the Son whose life, death, and resurrection bring reconciliation. Yet

10. For examples, see *The Church for Others,* pp. 95-126.

remaining is the sharing of the benefits of Christ's saving Work with the world, and thus the third mission, that of the Holy Spirit. Part and parcel of that mission is the pentecostal birth of the church here described, based on the account in the book of Acts. The third mission continues, as in the creedal narrative — the forgiveness of sin, the resurrection of the body, the life of the world to come.

When the *missio Dei* is lodged within the full Christian Story, it must include the diaconal accent with which it was associated in the 1960s but can by no means be limited to it. When the world's fall is taken into account, the full Story must be told, and with it the reconciliation not only sought but also wrought in a second mission, that of the Person and Work of the Son. Included as well, as in the present Person and Work of the Holy Spirit in bringing the church to be, must be the third mission of God, one that includes the fullness of its needed charisms — *kerygma, leitourgia,* and *koinonia,* as well as *diakonia.* Unless the "mission of God" is seen in this broader trinitarian sweep, it fails to tell the whole Story.

New Testament Images of the Church

We have already entered the realm of New Testament imagery (the Body of Christ) and begun to examine the "church as the image of the Trinity." We continue on that path, drawing on some New Testament images of the church and following our ecumenical injunction linking them to recent ecumenical thought on their relation to the Trinity. Paul Minear's notable exploration of the ecclesial images is a durable resource on the subject, having been honored by re-publication forty years after its appearance, in the series, *New Testament Library.*[11]

A cascade of those suggestive ecclesial figures he identifies includes "the people of God," "the body of Christ," the "temple of the Spirit," vine, flock, bride, and wedding party. The World Council of Churches' study in progress that aims to produce an ecumenical document on ecclesiology, *The Nature and Purpose of the Church,*[12] makes a case for the first three of

11. Paul Minear, *Images of the Church in the New Testament* with a Foreword by Leander Keck, New Testament Library, Leander Keck, ed. (Philadelphia: Westminster/John Knox, 2004).

12. Faith and Order Paper 181, *The Nature and Purpose of the Church* (Geneva: WCC/ Faith and Order, 1998).

these images indicating the trinitarian roots of the church's being, although any one of them includes references to or assumptions about the others. The value of this proposal is the linkage of the nature of the church to the tripersonal God, as noted in the previous discussion.

The most persuasive WCC case for a trinitarian analogue is in the image of "the church as body of Christ," referring thus to what it calls the "trinitarian dimension" of the Son:

> Through the blood of Christ, God's purpose was to reconcile humanity in one body through the cross (Eph. 2:11-22). This body is the body of Christ, the Church (Eph. 1:23). Christ is the abiding head of this body and at the same time the one who, by the presence of the Spirit, gives life to it. In this way, Christ who is the head of his body, empowering, leading and judging (Eph. 5:23; Col. 1:18), is also one with his body (1 Cor. 12:12; Rom. 12:5). The image of the Body of Christ in the New Testament includes these two dimensions, one expressed in Corinthians and Romans, the other developed in Ephesians.[13]

The allusions in Scripture to the church as the Body of Christ, and the usage of such in church teaching, make it not only a fertile source of theological commentary on the nature of the church but also a pointer to the specific relation of the second Person to the church's being. As the Body of Christ, it is drawn into the very triune life of God through the Person of the Son.

The role of the third Person has strong New Testament warrants and historic usage, represented in *The Nature and Purpose of the Church* by the image of "the church as Temple of the Holy Spirit," though an image to be used with some qualification:

> References to the constitutive relation between Church and Holy Spirit run through the whole New Testament witness. Nevertheless there is no explicit image for this relation. The imagery that comes particularly close to the figurative descriptions of this relation entailed in the New Testament, and renders it in a particularly appro-

---

13. *The Nature and Purpose of the Church*, p. 13. Note that the word "dimension" is used here in yet another sense than the proposal of the parallel between the Persons and the images.

priate way, is the imagery of "temple" and of "house." This is so because the relation of Spirit to the Church is one of indwelling, of giving life from within. . . . By the power of the Holy Spirit believers grow into a "holy temple in the Lord" (Eph. 2:21), into a "spiritual house" (1 Peter 2:5). Filled with the Holy Spirit they pray, love, work and serve in the power of the Spirit, leading a life worthy of their calling, eager to maintain the unity of the Spirit in the bond of peace (Eph. 4:1-3).[14]

As we focused earlier on the church as the community marked by the four signs of the Spirit, it follows that the church is, yet again, seen to be drawn into the triune Life Together through the Spirit of the Son.

While the WCC document presumes the relation of the first Person, the Father, to the church as a distinguishable "dimension" of the Trinity vis-à-vis the church, no mention is made of the word "Father" in correlating the first Person with the chosen image, "Church as the People of God." Is this because of the textual stretch in making this connection? A desire to minimize paternal imagery, given inclusive language concerns? Perhaps. More likely, however, is the assumption that the first Person can be associated with the term "God," and is done so liturgically, in historic doctrinal discourse and in Scripture, so summarized in the trinitarian greeting, "The grace of the Lord Jesus Christ, the love of God and the communion of the Holy Spirit be with all of you" (2 Cor. 13:13). Such usage gives the authors a warrant for indicating how the purposes of God in gathering a particular people signal the universal intent of the triune God to "bring the possibility of communion for each person with others and with God, thus manifesting the gift of God for the whole world."[15]

However, what little space is given to the work of the first Person deals essentially with the "people of God" in its pre-pentecostal manifestation, and thus points to the election of Israel vis-à-vis the church:

In the calling of Abraham, God was choosing for himself a holy people. The recalling of this election and vocation found frequent expression in the words of the prophets: "I will be their God and they shall be my people" (Jer. 31:33; Ez. 37:27; Hosea 2:3, echoed in 2 Cor. 6: 16; Heb. 8:10). Through the Word (*dabhar*) of God and the Spirit

14. *The Nature and Purpose of the Church*, pp. 14-15.
15. *The Nature and Purpose of the Church*, p. 13.

(ruah) of God, God chose and formed one from among the nations to bring salvation to all. The election of Israel marked a decisive moment in the realization of the plan of salvation. . . .[16]

Thus, "church" in its widest and longest sense is related to the Israel of the Old Testament, as has been asserted in the concept of the community of the elect, the *coetus electorum* held by some traditions within the church, or in strands of "anti-supersessionist" writing that construe the Christian community as prolongation into the Gentile world of the calling of Israel, and a partner in waiting with the Jewish people for the final gathering of the people of God.[17] While all the Persons are present and active in the gathering of this chosen people of God, it is important to acknowledge the mission of the Father in the biblical narrative as establishing a linkage of the church of Christ with the "chosen people."[18]

The integration of the images of the church with dimensions of the Trinity is, in fact, the relating of ecclesial figures of speech to the divine economy, the unfolding plan of God, the "economic Trinity." While the church of Pentecost comes to be at the post-ascension outpouring of the Spirit, and is thus associated directly with the mission of the third Person, *The Nature and Purpose of the Church* study helps us to see in its interpretation of the biblical images the Spirit's relation not only to the other Persons but to their missions. As "the works of the Trinity are one,"[19] so too are the different Persons of the immanent Trinity in perichoretic unity. This too is a relationship of ecclesiology to trinitarian teaching. That is, the images of the church as the Body of Christ, the Temple of the Spirit, and the people of God are all pointers to, mandates on earth for, and eschatological anticipations of the ultimate Life Together. The images not only suggest diverse dimensions of the triune God in economic action, but also the triune God's immanent being.

---

16. *The Nature and Purpose of the Church*, pp. 12-13.

17. On the former, see Louis Berkhof, *Systematic Theology* (Grand Rapids: Eerdmans, 1938), pp. 567 and *passim*, and on the latter, Jürgen Moltmann, *The Church in the Power of the Spirit: A Contribution to Messianic Ecclesiology*, trans. Margaret Kohl (San Francisco: Harper & Row, 1975), pp. 144-50.

18. See "The Covenant with Israel: Elective Action" in *The Doctrine of Revelation: A Narrative Interpretation*, Edinburgh Studies in Constructive Theology (Edinburgh: Edinburgh University Press, 1997 and Grand Rapids: Eerdmans, 1997), pp. 105-19.

19. The ancient "law of the Trinity."

And yet more. As mirroring the very intent of God for the world in the Christian story — a life together that mirrors the divine Life Together — the images also adumbrate the *purpose* of the church as well as its *nature*. So also the WCC summarizes "God's Purpose for the Church":

> It is God's design so to gather all creation under the Lordship of Christ (Eph. 1:10), and to bring humanity and all creation into communion. As a reflection of the Triune God, the church is called by God to be the instrument in fulfilling this goal. The Church is called to manifest God's mercifulness to humanity, and to restore humanity's natural purpose — to praise and glorify God together with all the heavenly hosts. As such, it is not an end in itself, but a gift given to the world in order that all may believe (John 17:21).[20]

The mission of the church so described is manifest in the marks and attributes of the church to be yet explored and to the signs of the Spirit in the Acts account of the Christian church's birth.

The Church as a Divine-Human Institution

The three images here explored illumine the being of the church as a divine-human institution. The relation to the Persons and missions of the Trinity, otherwise expressed, constitute the church in its divine being. While not in simple continuity with the Incarnation, given the imperfection in the Body of Christ that makes it impossible to be a simple counterpart to the perfect humanity of Christ and the initiating singularity of the Word enfleshed, the church has a dual nature in analogy with the Person who continues to live in his earthly Body. Already we are making use of one of the images to give attention to the human "underside" of the organism associated in a special way with the triune God.

Paul's employment of the image of "the body of Christ" in his Corinthian letter makes quite clear the humanity of the church, and that in two senses: its finitude and its sin. As finite, the church is an institution with its structures, processes, and components, all in a history with its sociological patterns and needs. Thus the figure of a body with its many parts does duty for the apostle in counseling an early congregation on the fact of di-

20. *The Nature and Purpose of the Church*, p. 15.

verse constituencies within the church and the need to honor their contribution to the life and work of the church. But the humanity of the church has to do with its sin as well as its sociology. The varied parts each claim too much for their respective charisms, reducing the church to their own particular organs within the body. But "if all were a single member, where would the body be?" (1 Cor. 12:19). So the sin of hubris that afflicts the human self makes its way into the divine society as its all-too-human underside. Thus the church is both the Body of Christ in continuity with his Person and, at the same time, the body of Christians in their finite and fallen state.

The church as Temple of the Spirit is a building "not made with hands" but erected by the power of the third Person of the triune God. At the same time, it is a structure with varied rooms occupied by companies of believers with feet of clay. As with the organs in the Body, so with the occupants of aforementioned spaces "under the steeple," each constituency has its charism and call that perform a visible, indeed institutional, service for its Lord. In doing so, the Corinthian curse makes its appearance, a pretension to be more than it is. As with the body of varied members, so with the Spirit's building of many rooms; the occupants of a given space are tempted to scale the structure back to fit their proportions alone. If the building were a single room, where would the Temple be? Sin as well as finitude marks its humanity.

The church as "the people of God" is a gathering brought to be in accord with the eternal purposes of the Father and so joined to the first Person of the Trinity. But it is a *people* of the earth, earthy, as much as it is linked to the things of heaven, a people *of God*. As humanly peopled, it is like the body and the temple, finite, a creature subject to the vicissitudes and necessities of its life in time and history. As such, it is as diverse as any people that constitute a sociological reality. And like much human variety whose history is marred by imperial claims, it is subject to the same temptations of overlordship. "Our people" claim to be *the* people, bearing the true stigmata "of God." The humanity of the church in its finitude and sin, as well as its paradoxical divine nature, as with the other images is also suggested by this biblical figure.

Significantly, the diversity pointed to in all these images can be correlated with the four pentecostal signs of the Spirit. The people of God gravitate to one or another of the actions of the third Person of the Trinity, gather in one or another of the spaces in the Temple, are drawn to steward one or another of the charisms within the Body. Such human proclivities, gifted though they be with the multiple graces of the Holy Spirit, carry with them the temptations that Paul encountered in the Corinthian congregation and throughout his ministry. We need the eye, the ear, the hands, the feet for the fullness of the body, and they are given by grace to that end. Yet "the eye cannot say to the hand, 'I have no need of you, nor again the head to the feet, 'I have no need of you'" (1 Cor. 12:21).

All three images in their divine aspect have implications for the "where" of the church. As the Body of Christ born on the day of Pentecost according to the purposes of the Father among this people by the descent of the Holy Spirit on this Temple, promises have been made. "I am with you always, to the end of the age" (Matt. 28:20). The "always" is a pledge made that the Spirit of the Son of the Father will never leave the apostolic community, a Presence that will continue to the end of the Story. Life will always flow in the Body signaled by the same signs of the Spirit — telling, celebrating, doing, and being.

One implication of the constant flow is that there will be no great gap between a New Testament community and the later life of this Body. The leap from the purity of the first Christians over the church's history to the repristination of that early presumed perfection among a chosen few is a sectarian impulse to be resisted. For all the countersigns of sin in the church catholic and continuing (sins from which that earliest assembly was itself not exempt), the "always" is a promise from the One who will keep faith with his people. Another implication is that "church" does not happen only when some unforeseen decision is made by an inscrutable God. Indeed the sovereign God can so choose to do, but such freedom *from* our expectations is always within the context of, and in relation to, the freedom *for* us manifest in the promises made. Thus there is the "already-always" of the Holy Spirit that constitutes the being of the church.

How the church in its divine nature is ever and again graced with the signs of the Spirit, yet subject in its human nature to its frailties in the stewardship of these mysteries, is manifest in the recent history of the churches as the readers of this study know them. As in Corinth, so in the congregation around the corner and the church at large in our time and place. To ground our doctrinal discerning of the signs of the Holy Spirit we turn next to an effort to discern the signs of our own times.

CHAPTER 2

Discerning the Signs of the Times

I n this encounter with the day-to-day work and witness within the church, we begin with the era of *Under the Steeple* and proceed to the present, with an eye open for the "signs of the Spirit" within the "signs of the times." While only rough in alignment, a decadal periodization of this history is used, one that corresponds to cultural developments in the West, the habitat of this ecclesiology.[1] We will look not only for the signs, but also for resistance to the work of the Spirit, the human as well as divine dimensions often manifest as the too-often tawdry underside of the Body of Christ.

In this narrative we will attempt to face squarely that "tawdry underside." Especially so, when we arrive at the state of the North American mainline Protestant churches at the beginning of the twenty-first century. No ecclesiology that rises out of that environment, as this one does, can fail to look with an honest eye at the problems discernible among us. The writer, living and working for all these decades in a denomination that was born at the mid-twentieth century, and has been virtually defined by the

---

1. It has become commonplace to identify cultural changes in North American society in terms of "the 50s," "the 60s," etc., recognizing the overlaps and "ideal type" character of such descriptions. For an early attempt to correlate cultural "rapidation" of this sort with theological developments, see the author's essay, "Theology: Ephemeral, Conjunctural and Perennial," in David W. Lotz, ed., *Altered Landscapes: Christianity in America, 1935-1985.* Essays in Honor of Robert T. Handy (Grand Rapids: Eerdmans, 1989), pp. 246-67.

tension between *relating* to, and *capitulating* to, the temper of the times, will draw on this life within United Church of Christ as well as comparable experience in the wider church. To this reality/Reality we now turn as the pastoral context for understanding the biblical text and classical teaching about Where and What the church is.

The 50s — *Koinonia*

The Church Local

"The 50s" — what a time to be in pastoral ministry! Not because of the conventional wisdom: haloed memories of filled sanctuaries and the building boom of suburban churches. Too easily forgotten in such retrospectives is the excitement of mission to estranged populations in an East Harlem Protestant Parish or the toughened ecclesiology of "the company of the committed" in the new Washington, D.C., "Church of the Saviour."

The temper of the 50s begins in this account in the late 40s. Under the guidance of the University of Chicago Federated Faculties teacher, James Luther Adams, and CIO education director-become professor, Kermit Eby, the author and spouse spent a 1948 summer studying "The Church and the Working Classes in Great Britain" with its high moment a week at the worker/pastor-created Iona Community in Scotland.[2] We came away from that summer with a sense of call to ministry with "the proletariat," convinced that the church could come alive and society change only through a frontier mission to the workers whose souls must be won (away from the Marxists), and whose bodies needed ecclesial allies in a struggle for justice. So came the choice to serve a Chicago stockyards district mission, Raymond Chapel, while completing doctoral studies at the University of Chicago Divinity School, learning for two years to walk the streets and visit the projects, preaching, teaching, baptizing, marrying, burying, and doing settlement house work with five students assigned to the mission from the Baptist Missionary Training School. No great equivalents of Saul Alinsky's organizing achievements in the nearby Back-of-the-Yards neighborhood,[3]

2. George F. MacLeod, *We Shall Rebuild: The Work of the Iona Community on Mainland and on Island* (Glasgow: Iona Community, n.d.).

3. So Saul D. Alinsky, *Reveille for Radicals* (New York: Random House, 1946).

but an intense life together with folk on the margins. The ministry was so consuming that little time was left for "book-learning," and thus a Fackre flunk in the key Ph.D. "field exams" at the University. The outcome was a sad resignation of the chapel ministry and return to full-time studies before moving on.

"Moving on," after a second go-around on the exams, this time successful, meant a search for full-time working-class ministry. So came a call to a debt-ridden and depressed charge in the Monongahela Valley of Greater Pittsburgh. The turn of the decade also meant a move from long-time Baptist affiliations into the Evangelical and Reformed Church whose ecumenical and sacramental identity cohered much more with our growing commitment to an "evangelical catholicity" in theology and an ecumenism born from our World Council of Churches assembly experience. The "E&R Church" also had a history of mission to industrial areas, with its luminary, Reinhold Niebuhr, one of our mentors, a practitioner of such in Detroit.[4]

Ten years of ministry in a two-point mission charge under the smokestacks of the steel mill towns of Homestead and Duquesne meant life in the midst of the era's strikes, layoffs, and industrial depersonalization.[5] During those years, however, so many joys and adventures with experiments in a storefront ministry for the Homestead congregation inspired by New York's East Harlem Protestant Parish, a "Milliron Community" begun in a tract of land and abandoned church modeled on Scotland's Iona Community, building debts paid off in Duquesne, a transition from the storefront to a first unit in Homestead's adjacent "workingman's paradise," West Mifflin, and the growth of the parish from seventy to seven hundred souls. The hymn written by Purd Deitz of the national mission board of the denomination caught the spirit of those days: "We would be building temples still undone. . . ."[6]

We had come to the Steel Valley, just as we had to the Stockyards district, with an instrumental view of our work in the congregation: the church exists to serve the workers in their socio-economic plight. However, in both cases, ministry in a congregation turned out to mean not only

---

4. In tribute to the same, the author's *The Promise of Reinhold Niebuhr* (New York: Lippincott, 1970) and the revised edition (Lanham, Md.: University Press of America, 1994).

5. See the writer's "What Is Dehumanization?" *Theology and Life* 4, no. 4 (November 1961): 292-94.

6. Purd E. Deitz, "We Would Be Building," *The Hymnal* (St. Louis: Eden Publishing House, 1941), p. 452.

solidarity with workers in the struggle for social change but also creating in the midst of it a *community* that represented the vision of life together so absent in those days of industrial dehumanization. Here in the congregation itself, the alienated could come to know the life together for which they were intended, but were denied in the economic, political, and social arenas. The foreground sign of the Spirit in the church local, therefore, became *koinonia,* a reflection, we believed of "the apostles'. . . fellowship."[7]

The Church at Large

The 50s in the wider church began for us, as it had in the church local, in the late 40s, with a husband-wife hitch-hike to Amsterdam, Holland, during the summer studies of mission to British workers. There in August, 1948, we participated in the aforementioned first assembly of the World Council of Churches, smuggled into the hall as camera carriers for a sympathetic journalist. "Man's Disorder and God's Design" was the theme, one contested by Karl Barth in a notable speech as Atlas-like human pretension, and defended in other fiery remarks by Reinhold Niebuhr as expressing the proper work of the church. But both agreed with the assembly's main purpose set forth on this world stage — the hope for healing of a fractured universal church, a *koinonia* signaled in the solemn final words of its Message: "We intend to stay together."[8]

Drawn with passion to the ecumenical vision, we were determined to attend the second World Council of Churches assembly held in Evanston, Illinois, in 1954, this time as "accredited visitors" and not gate-crashers. The theme — "Christ — the Hope of the World" — reflected the bold christocentricity of the time, and one that demonstrated the parallel between the quest for unity and mission on the larger landscape of the church and what was transpiring in our own ministry on the Monongahela River. The climax of the assembly was a rally of 100,000 people in Chicago Stadium, highlighted by the testimonies of the seven presidents of the World Council and theologian Georgia Harkness's hymn written for the

7. Out of this experience came *Under the Steeple,* and two years later, *The Purpose and Work of the Ministry: A Mission Pastor's Point of View* (Philadelphia: The Christian Education Press, 1959).

8. "The First Assembly of the World Council of Churches: Message," *Man's Disorder and God's Design: The Amsterdam Assembly Series* (New York: Harper & Bros., n.d.), p. 231.

occasion, "Hope of the World." From start to finish, hopes soared for a church united and uniting. For all of us, it seemed, *koinonia* became the watchword as we moved away from this heady gathering into our particular congregations "under the steeple."

Why this accent on "life together," one sign of the Spirit, in this period of history? The dominant theme in the social analysis of the time was the "depersonalization" of society, the "quest for community," and the desire in the post-war world of "organization man" and "the lonely crowd" for John and Jane Doe to find a name and a face. All this, as well, with the nation's apprehensiveness about "The Causes of World War III."[9] The church — local or universal — with its rallying cry of *koinonia*, appeared to be reading aright "the signs of the times."

The 60s — *Diakonia*

A life together in community, local or at large, could turn into an escape from the world, local or at large. Would *koinonia* prove to be retreat into pious conventicles insulated from society's miseries? The next decade told a different story, at least in the mainline churches.

The Church Local

"The Missionary Structure of the Congregation," "The Church for Others," "The Pastor and the World" . . . signature intellectual and action involvements of the times for the writer, and mandates for action by congregations. At the turn of the decade, 1961, we had moved from parish ministry to a long-anticipated teaching ministry, as I accepted a call to Lancaster Theological Seminary of the Evangelical and Reformed Church, determined to share with a new generation of seminarians the lessons learned on the ground. But this time it took shape as the pursuit of the vision of Martin Luther King, Jr., and with it came center stage the decade's accent on *diakonia*.

9. For names and themes in influential studies of the period see C. Wright Mills, *White Collar* (New York: Oxford University Press, 1951); *The Causes of World War III* (New York: Ballantine Books, 1959); Robert Nisbet, *The Quest for Community* (New York: Oxford University Press, 1953); William H. Whyte, *The Organization Man* (New York: Simon and Schuster, 1956); David Riesman with Nathan Glazer and Reuel Denney, *The Lonely Crowd* (Garden City, N.Y.: Doubleday & Co., 1953).

"The Missionary Structure" study was the project of the World Council of Churches that brought together a company of activist theologians and clergy from Europe and North America asked to explore the emergent "secular" theology that traced its recent roots to Dietrich Bonhoeffer's later writings and martyrdom. The new accent was on secular mission, not church unity — *diakonia,* not *koinonia.*[10] "Go into all the *world,*" "You are the light of the *world,*" "God so loved the *world*"; these were the biblical texts of the times for many of us. Ethicist Gibson Winter, part of the WCC study that called for participating in the sufferings of Christ out in the world in the arenas of "being, having, and belonging" (war, poverty, and race), judged the parish to be ill-equipped for such a mission, confined as it was to "women's programs" and "hatching, matching, and dispatching" (baptism, marriage, and burial). Following suit, a denominational campaign wrote on its banners "the world sets the agenda" (as juxtaposed to the decade's perceived focus on the church and its agenda).[11]

However, the same denomination that put to the fore the world's agenda, the UCC, decided on a sequel 1968-69 "biennial emphasis," "The *Local Church* in God's Mission." It did so as a counterpoint to the tendency of secular mission to imply, if it did not outright assert, that the congregation had to be replaced by "new forms" — coffee houses, industrial mission, campus ministries, metropolitan missioners, and "preaching from unexpected pulpits"[12] such as the deeds and words of the civil rights and peace movements, urban renewal efforts, creative film, theater, and fiction. However, some of us said, "let these new forms be *partners of,* not *replace-*

10. Leading lights in the North American Working Group of which the writer was part were Harvey Cox, Robert Spike, Gibson Winter, Andrew Young, Gordon Cosby, Letty Russell, Jitsuo Morikawa, Collin Williams, Jerald Jud, Howard Moody, George Webber. Not all were caught up in the secular theology of the hour, notably Markus Barth who came with a stinging critique of Gibson Winter's views within the Missionary Structure study group: "The Latest Church Ideology: A Review Article of Gibson Winter, *The New Creation as Metropolis,*" in *Christianity and Crisis* 22 (1962): 206-11.

11. Thus the popular study books of the day: Peter Berger's *The Noise of Solemn Assemblies* (Garden City, N.Y.: Doubleday & Co., 1961); Gibson Winter, *The Suburban Captivity of the Church* (Garden City, N.Y.: Doubleday & Co., 1961); Harvey Cox, *The Secular City: Secularization and Urbanization in Theological Perspective,* revised edition (New York: Macmillan, 1966); the series by Colin Williams, *Where in the World* (New York: National Council of Churches, 1963) and *What in the World* (New York: National Council of Churches, 1964).

12. The title of a series of secular literary excerpts published by an agency of the United Church of Christ.

ments for, the congregation." The North American and West European Working Groups of the World Council of Churches spent years investigating the "church for others,"[13] as did an outpouring of study books and theological interpreters — Harvey Cox, Peter Berger, Jitsuo Morikawa, Robert Spike, Collin Williams, and others. Then there were the practitioners who did in local venues what was being said by the front-line theology — Bill Webber, Archie Hargraves, and Letty Russell in the East Harlem Protestant Parish, Robert Raines in his Germantown, Pennsylvania, congregation, Gordon Cosby serving D.C.'s Church of the Saviour, Howard Moody in Judson Memorial Church on New York's Washington Square, Wallace Fisher in Trinity Lutheran Church, Lancaster, Pennsylvania.[14]

The momentum of steel valley ministry continued for us, but now redirected in the 1960s to the race, peace, and gender movements that overtook those of class. But with a difference, suggested earlier. Given our "Mercersburg theology" and its ecclesiology that did not dissolve the church into the world but affirmed the centrality of Word and sacrament, we argued determinedly for its primary home, the local congregation, and sought to link this "old form" with the needed "new forms."[15] A dissenter from the Winter line in the WCC study, writing on the relevance of the local church, I was called by the United Church of Christ to chair the 1968-69 Emphasis on the place of the local church in "God's mission," and asked by the UCC's Council for Christian Social Action to write a book that would help congregations find ways of keeping company with Christ in both church and world (the "room" and the "road" of Luke 24:28-32). Thus came *The Pastor and the World*[16] and with it the struggle to live out this ecclesiology as a family in working-class St. Luke's UCC, Lancaster, with a liturgical and sacramental practice similar to that of our former years. And

---

13. So the volume of its reports, *The Church for Others and The Church for the World* (Geneva: World Council of Churches, 1968).

14. So for example, Elizabeth O'Connor's *Call to Commitment: The Story of the Church of the Saviour, Washington, D.C.* (New York: Harper & Row, 1963); Robert Raines, *The Secular Congregation* (New York: Harper & Row, 1968), George William Webber, *The Congregation in Mission* (Nashville: Abingdon Press, 1964); Wallace Fisher, *From Tradition to Mission* (Nashville: Abingdon Press, 1965).

15. Argued in detail in "The Crisis of the Congregation: A Debate," in *Voluntary Associations: A Study of Groups in Free Societies*. Essays in Honor of James Luther Adams, ed. D. B. Robertson (Richmond, Va.: John Knox Press, 1966), pp. 275-97.

16. *The Pastor and the World* (Philadelphia: United Church Press, 1964).

to do it in partnership with the founding of an activist coffee house, "Encounter," closely affiliated with, and dependent upon, the area's thirty-nine UCC congregations. The coffee house became a base of operations for local and national marches and demonstrations, freedom schools, a struggle to integrate the city's junior high schools, and the founding of a citizens' newspaper alternative to the city's monolithic press, all rising from initiatives of local pastors and congregations.[17] It was, for many of us in the mainline churches, the Day of *Diakonia*.

The Church at Large

Already we have seen the impact of conciliar Christianity's secular-oriented themes as they affected the church local in all the ways described here, as in denominational and ecumenical venues. Yet the most dramatic exemplification on a world scale came in the second Vatican Council of the Roman Catholic Church. *Aggiornamento* — updating vis-à-vis the challenges of the modern world — was to the fore in that historic event. So too in other parts of the church universal, notably in the WCC study to which allusion has been made, and in its fourth assembly at Uppsala and succeeding ones in which "justice, peace, and the integrity of creation" were the dominant refrains. The image used by Pope John XXIII to characterize the second Vatican Council represented the foreground note of *diakonia* in this era: "opening a window to the world."

The world-orientation of Vatican II, of course, took many forms. Openness to the world of other Christians was a marked feature, including the presence of non–Roman Catholic Christian observers at the assembly.[18] Openness also to exploring the relation of Christian faith to world religions, with a commission created to facilitate the dialogue. The declaration on the apostolate of laity was a clear embodiment of the worldly accent, seeing its role principally as discipleship in the secular arena through lay vocations.

17. Detailed in various of the writer's books and booklets, as in *Secular Impact* (Philadelphia: Pilgrim Press, 1966) and *Second Fronts in Metropolitan Mission* (Grand Rapids: Eerdmans, 1968).

18. See Douglas Horton's *Vatican Diary* series (Boston: United Church Press, 1964, 1965, 1966) and also Theodore Louis Trost, *Douglas Horton and the Ecumenical Impulse in American Religion*, Harvard Theological Studies (Cambridge, Mass.: Harvard University Press, 2002).

And the entire direction of the Council, from its theological statements to its programmatic proposals, was a manifestation of the same kind of turn to the world as seen above, albeit in Roman Catholic idiom.[19] Surely, there was a sign of the Holy Spirit in this diaconal ferment of the time.

The 70s — *Leitourgia*

The Church Local

Church on Friday nights? That was the way it was done at Eliot Church, Newton, Massachusetts, a congregation named after the seventeenth-century missionary to Native Americans, and known for its passion for social mission. At the end of the 1960s the church's anti-war witness was symbolized by a coffin on the lawn that ended in an assault on attending members by a group of passing hardhats.

But then came a new turn in the 1970s, prompted by soul-searching as to how to sustain through the inner life of the church those wounded in the battles of the previous decade. *Leitourgia* was beginning to have its day. It took the form in this locale of Friday-night church — three hours designed for young and also other families "open to the future," comprised of meal, guitar music and interpretive dance, intense group discussion about topical justice and peace matters, a laid-back dialogue homily on the floor rather than from the high pulpit in the sanctuary, marching, and singing and swinging with banners and balloons — worship as "celebration." Eliot Church's innovations in worship were so representative of new trends that NBC sent a television crew to film them. Two of the Fackre children could be seen on the guitar and Dad had a spot interview to interpret the event theologically, while Mom's colorful banners and buttons were everywhere visible.[20] Eliot had a Sunday service also, for those whose consciousness

---

19. The Dulles volume cited above, *Models of the Church* (New York: Doubleday, 1978), is an interesting illustration of how a Roman Catholic thinker shaped at that time by the Second Vatican Council sought to hold together the various dimensions of the church, while giving attention to the foreground role of the "servant" accent: "We may welcome the current stress on the servant Church as a sign of spiritual progress. But the concept of service must be carefully nuanced so as to keep alive the distinctive mission and identity of the Church" (p. 95).

20. So "Banners Tell of a Festive Faith," *United Church Herald* 13, no. 8 (August 1970): 22-27.

was thought to be insufficiently raised to the level of the exciting new forms. However, even here new accents were not altogether absent, as the first four rows of pews were unhitched to form a hint of a church-in-the-round and encourage participative worship.

After the activist cum worship-innovating pastor left in 1971, an attempt was made to do a frontline experiment in congregational life that would include a "cathedral" church where all would worship, the old Eliot building, which would be used as a center for mission, and a third building — belonging to a congregation with declining membership — to be used as an educational center. But this venture in reconfiguration failed by vote of the cathedral congregation, which was not yet convinced it wanted to associate with the free-wheeling Eliot folk.[21] Out of the defeat arose a team of Eliot clergy members who pressed hard for the sale of the building and the removal of the congregation to an available Newton mansion where the "company of the committed" could live out its self-defined radical Christianity in free-form worship. As it turned out, wiser heads saw a future for the congregation in its present location, and their search committee found a pastor with a 60s social-action history, alert to the wider liturgical movement and its premises, steeped in classical theology and furnished with notable preaching skills.[22] During his twenty-year tenure, the Friday nights disappeared, worship in the sanctuary returned, albeit preaching from the people's floor, but now in the setting of an open-ended Mercersburg-style liturgy and vigorous social action, with the congregation re-grown in a determined evangelism outreach.

And *leitourgia* at the seminary? Quite conventional in its 1950s divided chancel, central "altar," cross, and aisle, with student and faculty preaching from the modestly raised pulpit until an upsetting event, one anticipating the 70s liturgical experimentation. The newest faculty member was regularly assigned worship responsibilities, and so I was asked to lead a week with students from the "senior seminar" designed to integrate at the end of studies all that had gone before and prepare the class for their forthcoming ministry of relevance and innovation. Soon there arose among the partici-

21. A vision sketched out in the writer's "COCU from the Ground Up," in *Andover Newton Quarterly* 12, no. 1 (September 1971): 34-41.

22. The Rev. Herbert Davis, coincidentally the leader of the civil rights movement in Lancaster in the 1960s and co-founder with the writer of the coffee house, Encounter, described in Gabriel Fackre and Herbert Davis, "Encounter and Pip's Place," *United Church Herald* 7, no. 4 (February 15, 1964): 17-19, 34.

pants the question: Why had not the cutting edge banner-button-and-balloon worship yet come to stuffy Andover Newton?

On a dark night, the seniors and their facilitator made their way with toolboxes into Colby Chapel and proceeded to unscrew all the pews, re-arranging them into a contemporary "church-in-the-round" worship space. The following morning before chapel time, the students and my banner-making spouse proceeded to cover all the walls with forty of her designs. As Dorothy was putting the finishing touches on the chancel hanging, the door opened and "Sarge," head of "buildings and grounds," burst into the sanctuary, looked up at the figure atop the ladder and shouted, "What are you doing to my chapel!" From her heights, the banner-maker looked down and responded in kind, "*Your* chapel?" Thus came "the week that was" in new prayer patterns for America's oldest seminary, with its participatory worship, professors and students eyeing each other cautiously across the space of the pews-in-the-round, student voices ringing to current guitar tunes, and a final free-wheeling eucharist.

Not long after that the pews returned, re-screwed, to their original location. They have stayed in place ever since. However, chapel services are not as they once were, for student initiative is now permanently in place. African American and Hispanic worshipers pick up the participatory accents in their own way, and a professor of liturgics is always on hand, seeking to bring the developments of the wider liturgical movement to bear on Andover Newton's hill. Indeed, banners are now part of the standard scene in chapel and throughout the campus.

The Church at Large

Depending on who one asks, the liturgical renewal movement goes back at least a half-century, possibly a century. Certainly a landmark was the Second Vatican Council. However, its impact on the latter church, and on others influenced by it, could be seen in the decade of the 1970s. In the Roman Catholic Church signs of change were visible that paralleled those cited earlier, but manifest in a different way: the recovery of liturgy as "the work of the people." Thus the Mass in native tongue, the altar brought off the wall and tabled down among the people, a participative liturgy, the elements in both kinds, congregational singing, a higher profile for preaching, and greater attention to Scripture.

Using the World Council of Churches as another sign of the times in the church at large, we see similar evidences of the liturgical renewal movement in reports from Faith and Order conferences and declarations at WCC assemblies. However, a small straw in the wind of a restiveness yet to come happened in 1968 at the fourth assembly in Uppsala, Sweden. While the report of one section, "Worship in a Secular Age," echoed both the activism of the 60s and the populism in worship of the 70s, there were questions raised by African and Asian voices, those who did not judge secularity to be the defining context as it appeared to be in the West with its influence on the worship issues. And at the same time in Roman Catholic venues, there was increasing restiveness with the new ways. To be continued.

While the *leitourgia* being explored here has been linked to the liturgical renewal movement in both its universal and local expressions, it is a theme that also encompasses broader developments in both the culture and the church. The decade saw the rise of "spirituality," a phenomenon very diverse in its expressions. In common with liturgical concerns, it represented a move to the "vertical" often away from the claimant "horizontal" issues of the 60s, sometimes to better support them among those exhausted by single-string activism, sometimes to articulate a both-and approach, sometimes to escape from the hardscrabble world of politics in what was thought to be the more real world of piety. And parallel again to the liturgical renewal movement, spirituality appeared in conjunction with a version of "the work of the people," or more specifically the attempt to honor the agenda of folk in the "now" rather than fall in line with a prescribed tradition from the past. Thus came experimentation with a variety of modes of prayer, contemplation, meditation, and worship; a growing interest among Christians and in popular culture with world religions, diversity being the order of a day, one that gave pride of place to the perceived needs of the people; and with all this the dramatic growth and higher visibility of Pentecostal traditions and forms of worship.

In local church setting for the writer, such experimentation arose in a 1970 stint as theologian-in-residence at the Church of the Crossroads in Honolulu, Hawaii. There it ranged from a free-flowing worship in the early service that anticipated the Newton experiences, all the way over to mid-Pacific novelties such as "giving sanctuary" to the Hare Krishna devotees on the church grounds, and listening with our teen children to their guru, Sai, hold forth in his evening love feasts, with one of our daughters briefly drawn into the circle of Krishna-ites because she believed they really understood "celebration."[23]

Insofar as the accent on *leitourgia* entailed a verticality that attempted to correct an earlier period's reductionist horizontality, the rise of *evangelism* in the mainline Protestant churches can be seen as of a piece with the direction of this decade. A national evangelism campaign sponsored mostly by evangelicals, "Key 73," seemed to signal an about-face from the activism of the 60s. Yet not all went the way of an either-or. So came to be the "Word in deed" movement of other mainline churches, one that began in the UCC at a 1972 Deering, New Hampshire, conference during which participants seized control of the denomination's agenda and produced a declaration that partnered word and deed, a text that became the charter of one of that church's boards.[24] The writer served as part-time consultant for several years to a reborn evangelism department, an agency that had been temporarily suspended in the fevers of the 60s.[25]

Leitourgia — in its narrow sense, and in its broadest meaning — new and different experiments in "the work of the people" as they turn their hearts to God in worship and the witness that grows out of it, yet another sign of the Spirit. Hearts? But what of minds? Loving God with the mind, the people's work of *theology* was yet to have its own day.

The 80s — *Kerygma*

The Church Local

The "Word" in the "Word in deed" evangelism movement of the 1970s was harbinger of church developments in the next decade. Congregations and clergy who participated in this conjunction knew that there was no au-

---

23. Guitarist daughter, Bonnie, is now a Lutheran pastor. Her journey was written up by her sister, Gabrielle, as "Dorothy and Hare Krishna" in Harriet Harvey, *Stories Parents Seldom Hear: College Students Write About Their Families* (New York: Dell Publishing Co., 1983).

24. The manifesto of "action evangelism" was the 1972 "Deering Statement of Commitment" drafted by the writer, to be found in Edward Powers, *Signs of Shalom* (Philadelphia: United Church Press, 1973), pp. 56-57.

25. Several of the writer's books took up these themes: *Do and Tell: Engagement Evangelism in the 70s* (Grand Rapids: Eerdmans, 1973) and *Word in Deed: Theological Themes in Evangelism* (Grand Rapids: Eerdmans, 1975).

thentic mission without a message spoken as well as acts of mercy and justice done. In the grassroots evangelism efforts of the time, the message came to be identified for many as "the story," echoing the language of hymns that ran from Colin Sterne's evangelical "We've a Story to Tell to the Nations" to Harry Emerson Fosdick's plea in "God of Grace and God of Glory" to "crown thy Church's ancient story," but also reflecting the growing attention to narrative in the theology of the period.[26] Thus came the formulation that sought to bring together the changing accents, as in the titles in a video training tape for pastors: "getting the Story in," "getting the Story out," and "getting the Story straight." The "in-ness" of conversion and the out-ness of a "do and tell" evangelism had to be grounded in clarity and conviction about the Christian story itself.[27]

Kerygma as proclamation of the gospel — what goes on in evangelization and also in preaching and teaching within the church — engages both the heart and the head. In this decade, pastors and people in congregations came to realize more and more the importance of the *content* of faith, the affirmations about life, death, and destiny entailed in the gospel. Especially so, as the press judged that the church to which I belonged, as well as other mainline denominations, had only a "pallid but personable faith."[28] Not a few in the churches began to say that while knowledge of things of the faith did not guarantee faithfulness to the gospel, without it there is no proclamation of the gospel. Solid Christian teaching is the necessary, though not sufficient, feature of a faithful community. Loving God with the mind is part and parcel of loving God.

Of course, *didache* is *teaching* the faith, the specificity of communicating the content of *kerygma,* and thus it is wrapped into proclamation. It was this mode of "getting the Story straight" that occupied much of the writer's work as professor of Christian theology at Andover Newton, but also in numerous pastor and laity conferences during the summers, and on the speaking circuit throughout each year. Parallel to these movements of the mouth came those of the pen. A mini-systematics that had come out in the late 70s became in a second edition in 1984 Volume 1 of this *Christian Story* series, followed in 1988 by Volume 2, both of them accom-

26. Notably in the "Yale school," but actually a much wider phenomenon. See the writer's "Narrative Theology: An Overview," in *Interpretation* 37, no. 4 (October 1983): 340-52.

27. Tapes by the writer produced by the United Church of Christ Board for Homeland Ministries.

28. "A Pallid but Personable Faith?" *Time,* September 29, 1980, p. 85.

panied by articles and essays in collections about one or another Christian doctrine.[29]

The need for clarity and conviction about the central teachings of the church became claimant in the mainline denominations. One form it took in the United Church of Christ was a grassroots effort by pastors to resist cultural trendiness and doctrinal indifferentism. This began for the writer in a 1977 gathering in St. Paul's UCC Church in Chicago on the state of the faith, out of which grew the "Biblical-Theological-Liturgical Group" that in its East Petersburg Declaration challenged

- the civil religion that tempts us to mute the uncivil Word of truth we may be called to speak;
- the techniques of management and manipulation on which we have relied in the Church that have elbowed aside biblical preaching, sound theological teaching, living worship and sacrament;
- the latest wisdom of this world that regularly beguiles us from our fundamental norms of Scripture and Tradition.[30]

It continued in the formation in 1983 of the Mercersburg Society, which sought to retrieve for the present church the theological, sacramental, and liturgical traditions of John Williamson Nevin and Philip Schaff.[31] High point of the decade was the creation in 1984 of the first Craigville Theological Colloquy on Cape Cod in Massachusetts, sponsored by the two aforementioned bodies, bringing together 160 pastors and laity from across the country to celebrate the fiftieth anniversary of the Barmen Declaration, and at its end sending a "Letter" to the churches of the denomination echoing the accents of that historic document:

Loyal to our founders' faith, we acknowledge Jesus Christ as our "sole Head, Son of God and Savior" (Preamble, Para 2, *The Constitution of*

29. *The Christian Story*, vol. 1, *A Narrative Interpretation of Basic Christian Doctrine*, 3rd edition (Grand Rapids: Eerdmans, 1996), and *The Christian Story*, vol. 2, *Authority: Scripture in the Church for the World* (Grand Rapids: Eerdmans, 1987).

30. See "The East Petersburg Declaration," in Barbara Brown Zikmund and Frederick Trost, eds., *The Living Theological Heritage of the United Church of Christ*, vol. 7 (Cleveland: Pilgrim Press, 2005), p. 333.

31. See the journal of the Mercersburg Society, *The New Mercersburg Review*, for their continuing influence.

the United Church of Christ). With Barmen we confess fidelity to "the one Word of God which we have to hear and which we have to trust and obey in life and death (Barmen art. 1). Christ is the Center to whom we turn in the midst of the clamors, uncertainties and temptations of the hour.

We confess Jesus Christ "as he is attested for us in Holy Scripture" (Barmen art. 2). As our forebears did, we too "look to the Word of God in the Scriptures" (Preamble, Para 2). Christ speaks to us unfailingly in the prophetic-apostolic testimony. Under his authority we hold the Bible as the trustworthy rule of faith and practice. We believe the ecumenical creeds, the evangelical confessions, and the covenants we have made in our churches at various times and places, aid us in understanding the Word addressed to us. We accept the call to relate the Word to the world of peril and hope in which God placed us, making the ancient faith our own in this generation "in honesty of thought and expression and in purity of heart before God" (Preamble, Para 2).[32]

If this was a sign of the times — the teaching substance of preaching — then the backbone of *kerygma* was stiffening, even in a church said to be in theological disarray.[33] And the colloquies continued, albeit not without their critics fearful that attention to doctrine would deflect from the action agenda of the church.[34]

Indications kept coming that theological solidity was getting a hearing in officialdom. In that same church a Thank Offering Project was launched on discerning the theological commitments of the denomination, the earlier-cited *The Living Theological Heritage of the United Church of Christ* series was begun,[35] and the UCC was invited back into the Lutheran-Reformed negoti-

---

32. *The Living Theological Heritage,* vol. 7, pp. 334-39.

33. The president of the United Church of Christ, Avery Post, attending the event was quoted in a Religious News Service story in *Christianity Today* as saying about the Craigville Declaration, "I thank God for such a work." "United Church of Christ Members Want to End Theological Disarray," *Christianity Today,* July 13, 1984, p. 35.

34. On the critics, see Al Krass, "Evangelism, Social Action," *Seventh Angel* (September, 1984): 22-23. The colloquies have continued annually — XXIII in 2006 — now considered by many the most important theological forum in the denomination with grassroots as well as well-known presenters, weeklong conversation and worship, and an occasional colloquy declaration reported in the wire services.

35. Completed in 2005.

ations toward full communion, having been dropped out for a period because it was seen to be theologically incoherent and/or uninterested.[36]

The recovery of theological nerve was paralleled in this decade by the rediscovery of the importance of preaching. Journals on preaching came into being, lectionary aids appeared in abundance, and the homily as a teaching moment came into greater prominence.[37] Theologians were recruited to make their contributions to the homiletical task as the partnership of preaching and theology was nurtured.[38]

The Church at Large

By showing above the relation of supra-congregational movements and institutions to the church local we have already moved to proclamatory advances in the church at large. But beyond the denomination there were currents in the 1980s that paralleled and gave support to the efforts of the church local and national to lift up *kerygma*. Again, the World Council of Churches, in the form of its Faith and Order Commission, gave stunning evidence of revitalization in the arena of Christian teaching. After years of study the Commission set forth in 1982 its *Baptism, Eucharist and Ministry* "convergence" document.[39] In its wake were responses from national churches around the world, enough to fill six succeeding volumes. Theology, indeed important aspects of ecclesiology, came front and center in ecumenical circles.

On the heels of *BEM*, the same Commission produced a provisional version in 1987 of *Toward a Common Expression of the Apostolic Faith,* an appropriation for our time of the Nicene Creed. With reactions received to the same, the finished document was set forth in 1990 by the Apostolic Faith Steering Group. Though not receiving the attention given the *BEM*

36. Documented in Keith F. Nickle and Timothy F. Lull, eds., *A Common Calling: The Witness of Our Reformation Churches in North America Today* (Minneapolis: Augsburg Fortress, 1993). I was pleased to be part of all of these efforts at retrieving the tradition and re-grounding the mission in its theological foundations.

37. As for example the journal *Preaching*, Michael Duduit, editor.

38. *Lectionary Homiletics* being a notable journal, David Howell, J. Nichols Adams, and J. Andrews Edwards, eds. See also Roger E. Van Harn, ed., *The Lectionary Commentary: Theological Exegesis for Sunday's Texts,* 3 vols. (Grand Rapids: Eerdmans, 2001).

39. World Council of Churches, Faith and Order Commission, *Baptism, Eucharist and Ministry,* Faith and Order Paper No. 111 (Geneva: World Council of Churches, 1982).

document, "Confessing the Faith" was a landmark in ecumenical convergence, and a showcase of the revival of the kerygmatic cum theological calling of the church.[40]

Again, on a world scale, though not lodged in ecclesial structures, was "the resurgence in systematic theology" in this decade.[41] Thus came an outpouring of books and the launching of multi-volume series on constructive theology/systematic theology/dogmatics. These represented a recovery of full-orbed Christian teaching in the church's schools that paralleled the quest in congregations to be steeped in the basics, and the search for convergence on the essentials in world Christianity.[42] And publishing houses that risked serious theological works, notably Eerdmans, experienced healthy readership response and approbation from both ecclesial and academic circles.

Not a systematic work as such, but one of the most influential books among both teachers and pastors in this decade, was *The Nature of Doctrine* by George Lindbeck.[43] Out of the author's ecumenical experience, he asked how the notable convergences appearing at the time could be accounted for. (Lindbeck was an instrumental figure in bringing to be the later Roman Catholic–Lutheran *Joint Declaration on the Doctrine of Justification*.) His attention to the cultural-linguistic construal of doctrine (not to the exclusion of its propositional weight as critics wrongly contended), and tacitly to the importance of community theological self-definition, represented the stress on the importance of theology in this era.

The focus on *kerygma* in the 1980s had, as did the earlier accents, its historical context. The Introduction to the first volume in this series put it this way:

Both the confusions and the possibilities of this particular time and place warrant the telling and the hearing [of the Story]. The din of

40. World Council of Churches Faith and Order Commission, *Confessing the One Faith: An Ecumenical Explication of the Apostolic Faith as It Is Confessed in the Nicene-Constantinopolitan Creed (381)*, Faith and Order Paper No. 153 (Geneva: WCC Publications, 1991).

41. The title of an issue of *Interpretation*, 49, no. 3 (July 1995).

42. As noted, I surveyed this development in various journal articles, and did a study on the resurgence with seminary systematics professors, giving the result in a presidential address for the American Theological Society.

43. George A. Lindbeck, *The Nature of Doctrine: Religion and Theology in a Postliberal Age* (Philadelphia: Westminster Press, 1984).

competing religious claims perplexes both the seeker and the ordinary churchgoer. New cults, movements, and religious superstars appear almost daily on the television screen and the street corner to hawk their wares. The pious novelty may carry the label "Christian" or very self-consciously reject that identity and offer in its place either a secular nostrum or some import from the East. Who are we vis-à-vis these things, and how do we sort and sift their contentions? Confusion is compounded by the hard ethical choices moderns must make, from abortion and euthanasia, ecology and energy, to racial and ethnic justice, hunger, poverty, and war. While one cannot draw a straight line from basic Christian beliefs to particular stands on these questions, a knowledge of the Christian Story illumines them and points in a direction where answers can be found.[44]

Thus the kerygmatic sign of the Holy Spirit was a response to the increasing appearance and passions of alternative worldviews, and therefore a time for the mainline churches to tell their own Tale.

*   *   *

We break off at this point our pilgrimage through the periods. The time of the 90s and into the present century has been marked by the persistence of the legacy of one or another of the decades' accents. The stewards of a church constituted essentially as *koinonia,* or *diakonia,* or *leitourgia,* or *kerygma* are everywhere apparent. When we examine the present state of the mainline churches, they will continue to appear.

At the same time can be seen dissatisfaction with partialities and a search for the *fullness* of the work of the Spirit. Implicit in the emergence of one or another ecclesial motif was a sorrier underside. The high visibility of a given accent, while responsive to the issues of an era, is also a judgment on its overall state, for it discloses a previous inattention that had to be rectified. And yet again, the receding of that sign of the Spirit in a subsequent era of a new and different foreground accent was, and continues to be, ecclesially reductionist. Further, when one sign of the Spirit becomes the be-all and end-all of the church's life and witness, the fullness of ecclesial reality is reduced, overtaken by the faddish tendency to be driven and defined by the questions of a decade. Such reductions produce a hun-

---

44. *The Christian Story,* vol. 1, p. 1.

ger for wholeness. In passing, some reactions are noted, before an attempt is made here to develop an alternative to a reductionist ecclesiology.

One reaction comes from those who, judging the changing colors of the mainline flag, or its fixation on one or another cultural charge, to be a departure from the wholeness of its historic witness, simply choose to leave. But where to go? Recent decades have seen high-profile conversions from mainline Protestantism to both Roman Catholicism and Eastern Orthodoxy, as such ancient Christian traditions were seen to be keepers of full faith.[45] Also much in evidence were and are the movement of mainliners into one or another form of evangelicalism. The interesting convergence of "evangelicals and Catholics together"[46] is related to a shared reaction to developments in mainline Protestantism, its perceived cultural accommodation on both ethical and theological issues. Also notable are small trends out of evangelicalism and on the path toward both Rome and Constantinople, representing a search for catholicity (as "universality") in signs of the Spirit. And movements within mainline Protestantism from one communion to another show a similar longing for a more than single-sign ecclesiality. Dissatisfaction with mainline Protestantism's direction is taking an increasingly organized form in the alliance of self-described "renewal" movements, both urging a strong voice of dissent while staying within their present denominations and exploring congregational property issues if schism is seen as a possibility.[47] Also getting attention are new configurations that go under the label of "the emergent church."[48] In all these responses to mainline church failures there are learnings, calls to rethink and

45. Well known in America are Richard Neuhaus, a Roman Catholic convert, and Jaroslav Pelikan, an Eastern Orthodox convert, both from Lutheranism. For an apologia by an Episcopal-to-Roman Catholic convert, see R. R. Reno, "Out of the Ruins," *First Things* 150 (February 2005): 11-16.

46. A movement sired by Neuhaus and Charles Colson.

47. For a survey and support of such see Thomas C. Oden, *Turning around the Mainline: How Renewal Movements Are Changing the Church* (Grand Rapids: Baker Books, 2006).

48. Variously analyzed in magazines of both ecumenical and evangelical readership as in Scott Bader-Saye, "The Emergent Matrix," and Jason Byassee, "New Kind of Christian," *The Christian Century* 121, no. 24 (November 30, 2004): 20-31, and Andy Crouch, "The Emergent Mystique" and "Emergent Evangelism," in *Christianity Today* 48, no. 11 (November 2004): 37-43. For a critique of this phenomenon see D. A. Carson, *Becoming Conversant with the Emerging Church* (Grand Rapids: Zondervan, 2005), and for an interesting evangelical interchange about it and the movement see "The Emergent Church Conversation," *Reformation and Revival* 14, no. 4 (2005): 135-73.

redo its ecclesiology, but rethink it and redo it not by departures or intro-versions, but learning again in its own historical context from the New Tes-tament signs of the Spirit about the unity, sanctity, catholicity, and apostoli-city that Christ wills for his Body on earth.

Before we turn to that option in ecclesiology, an attempt at an honest look at the present circumstances of the church is in order. Again, personal narrative is part of the account of the circumstances described.

The State of the Church at Century's Dawn

Philip Jenkins has made a case for the dramatic growth and vitality of Christian churches in Africa, Asia, and South America. In his projections by 2050, the dominant form of the faith will not be the Christianity of the West but that of the global "other."[49] Indeed they account for the presence and striking growth of the Christian faith in the most hostile of religious environments — Muslim, Buddhist, and Hindu.

While it is customary to note that the "new Christendom" appears to take unconventional form in "Jesus movements," house churches, and Pentecostal expressions, the test by the standards of this inquiry is the state of the "signs of the Spirit" — *kerygma, diakonia, leitourgia, koinonia* and their relation to the classic attributes of unity, sanctity, catholicity, and apostolicity. Students of the explosion of Christianity in the global south, and in places of high peril for Christian believers, find that supportive life together, radical care for the helpless and hurt and a servanthood in the largest sense of suffering and death for one's beliefs, and vital worship and biblical conviction are key to evangelization in these contexts.[50] While all

49. Philip Jenkins, *The Next Christendom: The Coming of Global Christianity* (New York: Oxford University Press, 2002), and *The New Faces of Christianity: Believing the Bible in the Global South* (New York: Oxford University Press, 2006). For a distinction between a criti-cized "global Christianity" and what the author describes as a more authentic growing "World Christianity" in these regions, see Lamin Sanneh, *Whose Religion Is Christianity?* (Grand Rapids: Eerdmans, 2003).

50. Documented in the running reports and commentary of *Mission Frontiers,* pub-lished by the U.S. Center for World Mission under the leadership of Ralph Winter. The one hundredth anniversary of modern Pentecostalism prompted issues of both *The Christian Century* and *Christianity Today* in which its remarkable growth, its future challenges, and also its problems and darker side are taken into account. *The Christian Century* 123, no. 5 (March 7, 2006) and *Christianity Today* 50, no. 4 (April 2006).

that grows glitteringly, however, may not be gold, as a spate of critics have argued, it is difficult to challenge the correlation between these signs and the vital place of Christian witness, yesterday and today.[51]

We turn from the wider world to the arena being explored as the context for this study of the doctrine of the church, the "mainline church" just reviewed by decade. Its description in these latter days as the "oldline church," or even the "sideline church," suggests its present condition. Even more in the mode of indictment is that of R. R. Reno, who counseled us to learn to live *In the Ruins of the Church.*[52] He did so then, of course, knowing that there is more to the church than meets the sociological eye, a conviction about the theological nature of the church that we shall also pursue. But honesty about where we stand through the eyes of sight, before we look at the same phenomenon through the eyes of faith, honors the earthly dimension of this divine-human institution, especially so its *peccator* aspects. How then goes it with the signs of the Spirit (and thus the attributes and marks of the church in correlation with the same)? We shall blend the local and the "at large" in what follows, using as a portent of what is to come the sequel to the earlier narrative above.

The world has had its way with the Steel Valley. The long 1959 strike was a straw in the wind. For all the benefits secured by the steelworkers' union for those left with jobs after the inroads of automation, it was the beginning of the end of Big Steel along the Monongahela River. Today the location of the world's then-largest steel mill, and the site of the historic Homestead steel strike, is a moonscape. New technologies, overseas competition, shortsighted management, and more spelled the end of the historic center of steelmaking. Coterminous with the destruction of the mills and the loss of a hundred thousand valley jobs was the rise of crime and drugs. Duquesne has fared no better, its own deterioration hastened by an ill-conceived downtown rehabilitation program that demolished its main street and environs but never had the funds to replace them.[53]

---

51. As in David F. Wells, *No Place for Truth; or, Whatever Happened to Evangelical Theology?* (Grand Rapids: Eerdmans, 1993). See also Roger Olson, "Pentecostalism's Dark Side," *The Christian Century* 123, no. 5 (March 7, 2006): 27-30.

52. R. R. Reno, *In the Ruins of the Church: Sustaining Faith in an Age of Diminished Christianity* (Grand Rapids: Brazos, 2002). Reno, in spite of the thesis of this book, concluded that the ruins were unlivable and announced his conversion to the Roman Catholic Church.

53. For a realistic recent picture of the steel mill towns in which we served, see William Serrin, *Homestead: The Glory and Tragedy of an American Steel Town* (New York: Random

And what of the hope for a ministry to the proletariat? The year 2003 saw the close of the Homestead/West Mifflin congregation on the fiftieth anniversary of the construction of its promise-filled "first unit." Steelworkers are long gone from this mission in Workingman's Paradise, the seven members left on the last day transferring to the Duquesne congregation. And this sister church? Still soldiering on with part-time pastoral ministry and a loyal core of mostly mill retirees left after the removal of the steel works — not a few, happily, from the bulging youth groups of the missionary 50s. Survival of a congregation here is a not un-notable fact, as a block away one of the largest Protestant churches in Duquesne of another day, First Methodist, closed its doors at the turn of the twenty-first century.

And the Milliron experiment? The old chapel rebuilt in the late 50s by the hundred folk from the two congregations that made up the Milliron Community is still there, yet again refurbished, and now the center of a retreat area for the UCC's Penn West Conference, complete with website and steering committee. No longer the venue of pioneers from the Homestead-Duquesne charge, however, as the cabins in the woods are now derelicts or torn down, but, for all that, still alive in a new way in service for and to the Body of Christ.

And what of Raymond Chapel on 31st and Halsted Streets in Chicago, yet another mainline mission to the workers? A house afire, as we discovered in a recent visit to the old building. But now it has a different signboard out front signaling the new flames of a Pentecostal congregation. Inside we met the vital woman pastor who showed us around rooms bustling with young and old, speaking in tongues both ethnic and ecstatic.

"Where have all the flowers gone, long time ago?" No, not all gone, but rather, new ones. Do they look like those sprouting in the two-thirds world? Are they coming up right in the midst of "the ruins"?

Koinonia

The discussion at the 2004 annual congregational meeting of South Congregational Church, UCC, Centerville, Massachusetts (where the writer is a member) was intense. The presenting issue was the denomination's "God

---

House, Vintage Books, 1992, 1993). Interestingly, there are currently signs of revitalization in historic Homestead, but not so Duquesne.

Is Still Speaking" identity and advertising campaign, soon to become a national news story itself. The focus of the animated exchange, however, was on the latest phase of "GISS" — the drive with its goal of a 30-million-dollar television commercial campaign over the next two years, the first ad, seen on the denomination's website, scheduled for Advent, 2004. The thirty-second spot portrayed two hefty "bouncers" at a church door excluding all sorts and conditions — a gay couple, minority persons, the disabled, etcetera — juxtaposed to what was implied to be a representative UCC congregation, one that joyfully welcomed all those rejected by other churches. The ad, with its comparison of the UCC to others, seemed mean-spirited to many at the meeting, as did its predecessor in-house ads featuring the things the denomination did not believe and do ("no dogma . . . no rules" appeared to be at cross-purposes with the congregation's own strong commitment to classical Christian teaching, the ecumenical spirit of the founders of the UCC, and clear norms for Christian behavior).

The late October meeting was prescient of December events on a larger scale. The bouncer ad was rejected by CBS, NBC, and a portion of the ABC networks, though accepted by other outlets and stations. The reasons given by the networks, though couched in the language of "controversial," appeared to be the demeaning of other religious institutions as suggested by the bouncer imagery. However, the turndown was interpreted differently in a series of television interviews with UCC officials. The refrains were: the networks are violating free speech, freedom of religion, FCC fairness doctrine; were hypocritical, given their broadcast of gay-affirming secular programming; were displaying cowardice before the Bush administration with its right-leaning policies and the powerful new political fundamentalists with their "morality" agenda. Thus, the ad producers got a rush of free publicity around the country that they could never have dreamed of, and further affirmation for the courage of bucking the feckless media establishment.[54]

54. There were other media critics and religious voices that had a different interpretation of both the network rejection and the rationale of UCC personnel in producing the much-discussed first ad. Thus Peter Steinfels in a "Religion and Advertising" piece, December 18, 2004, in *The New York Times*. Again Joe Laconte's "Exclusion and Embrace," in *The Wall Street Journal,* December 3, 2004. So also Ted Olsen, "The Story Behind the TV Network's UCC Ad 'Ban.'" Weblog: *Christianity Today* 12, no. 2 (2004). An interesting exchange between Chris Matthews and an official of the UCC occurred in a December 3, 2004, MNBC interview in which Matthews pressed questions raised about UCC hubris and the invidious comparison between itself and other religious institutions. Additional money was not forth-

Important theological issues were raised for the church by the disputed ad and the campaign behind it. The media and general religious commentary about the Advent ad, pro and con, could not see from the thirty-second spot the premises of the larger and longer GISS campaign. As such, they speak volumes about the state of *koinonia* in a representative sector of the mainline Protestant churches.

The denomination in question, as in its name, United Church of Christ, began in 1957 as a union of four diverse Reformation traditions (Congregational, Christian, Evangelical, Reformed). So came its defining New Testament text "that they all may be one" (John 17:21) and chosen motto, "united and uniting." The UCC was seen to be an ecclesial existence born to witness to the church's attribute of unity, and sign of the Spirit's gift of *koinonia,* a long travel from there to the present marketing self-definition. The two are linked insofar as the loss of half of the church's membership in the intervening years eventuated in the advertising strategy whose niche ad theory eventuates in a "divided and dividing" self-definition in sharp contrast to its "united and uniting" originating intentions.

The campaign's symbol of a comma began to appear alongside of, and seemed often to replace, the official logo of the UCC — a cross and crown over the globe (already under fire for suggesting an unacceptable Christian imperialism) — and with it came a slogan borrowed from the comedienne Grace Allen: "Don't place a period where a comma belongs." The promoters of the campaign saw the symbol and slogan to be in continuity with the saying of Pastor John Robinson, as he bid farewell to the Pilgrims on their way to new lands: "God hath more truth and light to break forth from his holy Word." Most important, it interpreted the symbol, slogan, and assertion of new light and truth as representative of the true identity of the denomination, one that distinguished it from other churches. Thus one declared that the UCC is "about justice. . . . Not dogma. Not rules." Another proclaimed it is about "rights . . . not rites." Another rewrote a Christmas carol as "O Come all ye faithful, powerful and privileged . . ." juxtaposing it to "God invites all the faithful, so do we — the United Church of Christ." This identity gave the UCC a "niche" in the competitive market of North American reli-

---

coming for planned Advent and Lenten 2006 TV ads, but one was funded for the weeks preceding Easter 2006, with the similar theme of distinguishing the UCC from other churches, this time by a portrayal of the undesired in them being sprung up and out of their pews, rather than bounced down and out of their doors. The ads were again rejected by the major networks but did appear on some cable channels.

gion, a large one, it was assumed, because the very culture of late modernity was averse to rigidities, tradition, and in particular, absolutes of any kind. Especially inviting was this approach, since it stood in sharp contrast to alternative religious products, identified as they were with periods, not commas, and attachment to old truths and old lights. As in the selling of soap, so in the selling of religion, claims to superior achievement are seen to be integral to effective marketing. The high visibility in the United States of the Religious Right, especially its influence on the 2004 elections, provided a timely enemy product for a seasonal appeal to a "blue state" audience.[55] It was also noted by some that discontented Roman Catholics, passing through their church's sexual scandals and restiveness with the perceived imperial posture of its hierarchy, were a likely market for UCC outreach.[56]

The campaign moved into high gear in December 2004 with nationwide television advertising. However, an initial 4 million planned for the project was not forthcoming from donors so the Advent effort had to settle for a 1.6-million-dollar season of advertising, a portent of things to come as the campaign continued to falter.

The theological lesson of this venture is more revealing than the lack of support. It is the story of a church born to witness to ecclesial *koinonia*, and thus unity, as a decisive attribute of the church. It is the tale of travel from a church "united and uniting" to an image projected on the national screen in the colors of differentiation rather than unification (so a headquarters banner proclaiming, "Our unity is our diversity"), and of ecclesial *hubris* rather than humility. Given the image of a church purporting to be interested in exploration and diversity of viewpoint rather than "dogma," the new direction also has implications for the presence of the kerygmatic sign of the Spirit; and the accent on "rights, not rites" adversely affects the sign of *leitourgia* and thus the mark of eucharistic catholicity. Even the commitment to putting *diakonia* to the fore in the stress on justice and di-

---

55. The election map division of the country into liberal coastal blue states and heartland red states was a commonplace of this period.

56. An RNS reporter alluded to this statement in a report of a meeting on the Still Speaking campaign, but was forced to retract it by church authorities who claimed otherwise. Later the election of Cardinal Ratzinger, with an "enforcer" history in his decades as Prefect of the Congregation for the Doctrine of the Faith, as Pope Benedict XVI, provided an ideal opportunity to portray the UCC as the alternative to such retrograde religion. See Richard Ostling's citation of such in "Conservatives See Win in Rise of New Pope," April 23, 2005, AP wire service story.

versity sounds less persuasive when conjoined to the postmodern ad announcing that the UCC has "no rules."

Kerygma

And now fifty years later, what of *kerygma?* Are the statistics of a recent study of belief in God in mainline churches believable? Those who declared themselves to have "unwavering trust that God exists": 53 percent in the United Church of Christ and the Presbyterian Church? 56 percent in the Episcopal Church? 65 percent among Methodists, Disciples, Brethren, and Reformed?[57] A window into our mainline souls that may be revealing in this matter is the response of more than a few to the defining twenty-first-century event of the culture to which this volume seeks to speak, "9/11."

The attack on the Twin Towers brought in its wake a religious response throughout the nation. Marking the event were joint services made up of a variety of the religious groups in a given community. Compassion for the victims was a common theme. On what grounds were those diverse traditions taking part? The echo of Islam's call from the muezzin could be heard in the mullah's petition for peace, declaring unequivocally that "there is one God and Mohammad is his prophet." So also the clear witness to the one God of Abraham, Isaac, and Jacob was heard in the rabbi's intercessions. No doubt, either, was left in the minds of the worshipers about the specific groundings of the Buddhist priest. And the mainline Protestant pastor? In more than a few cases, in the services themselves, and often in the literature sent from denominational headquarters, all references to Christian particularity were excised. No prayers were to be made "in Jesus' name," for such prayers violated the rules against religious imperialism in our pluralist society.

Ironies abound in the veto of particularity among acceding mainline church figures. For one, insistence on the withdrawal of reference to the specifics of one's own faith is an implicit denial to other religions of their own particularist claims, indeed an adoption of a modern ideology of common core religion or a postmodern skepticism about the accessibility of ultimate truth. For another, it leaves silent the Christian warrant for compassion and peace, at a time when all the other participants did not

---

57. "America's Belief in God Is High but Nuanced," *The Christian Century* 121, no. 25 (December 14, 2004): 13.

hesitate to make clear their own religious claims. Mainline representatives who took the pluralist tack in this defining moment gave us a glimpse into the current state of *kerygma* in its ranks.[58]

As revealing as the statistical and anecdotal evidence is a study of a broader swath of church life, one that illustrates the linkage of the Spirit's sign of *kerygma* with the foregoing sign of *koinonia*. Cases in point: the little attention given to the landmark 1991 World Council of Churches' Faith and Order document, *Confessing the Apostolic Faith;* and the eight years that have passed without finalization of the 1998 Faith and Order Commission's document *The Nature and Purpose of the Church,* touted as "a stage on the way to a common statement," the lackluster response to both being in sharp contrast to the widespread official responses to the 1982 convergence document, *Baptism, Eucharist and Ministry.*

What this says by implication about that state of *kerygma* in ecumenical circles is declared openly in yet another study document published "without authority" by a group of theologians from diverse traditions, some young, and others being ecumenical veterans, *In One Body Through the Cross: The Princeton Proposal for Christian Unity.*[59] We shall return to this study subsequently, but some summary themes are here apropos. The organizers of the study preface the work with this sobering judgment:

> The wisdom of the first general secretary of the World Council of Churches, Willem Visser 't Hooft, "The World Council of Churches is either a christocentric movement or it is nothing at all," now carries little weight. Perhaps most distressing, the churches that once principally carried the movement have turned their energies to other matters, often to their own internal divisions.[60]

The sponsors were interpreting these conclusions of the study group:

> In the past, the National Council of Churches of Christ in the USA and the World Council of Churches have been important ecumenical agents. In recent years, they have become increasingly irrelevant to

---

58. For this argument, see Gabriel Fackre, "Claiming Jesus as Savior in a Religiously Plural World," online *Journal of Christian Theological Research* 8 (2003) reprinted as Chapter 1 in Volume 4 of this series.

59. Carl Braaten and Robert Jenson, eds., *In One Body Through the Cross: The Princeton Proposal for Christian Unity* (Grand Rapids: Eerdmans, 2003).

60. Braaten and Jenson, *In One Body Through the Cross,* p. 6.

the pursuit of unity, as political and social agendas have pushed aside concern for unity in the confession of faith and in the sacraments.[61]

The Fackre experience of the World Council and attraction to it, as noted above, included its political and social agenda — its passion to address "Man's Disorder" — but not to the exclusion of its christocentric commitment and its grounding in "the confession of faith and in the sacraments." The study concludes that this connection has been sundered, one replacing the other.

These ecumenists had their own solution, also citing developments that, in an albeit faltering way, continue to show signs of its presence: the 1961 declaration of the ecumenical vision at the third assembly of the World Council of Churches in New Delhi, India,[62] a call for Christian unity

> made visible as all in each place who are baptized into Jesus Christ . . . are brought by the Holy Spirit into one fully committed fellowship, holding the one apostolic faith, preaching the one Gospel, breaking the one bread. . . .[63]

And further,

> The churches' retreat from this vision is sin, which is visited upon the churches in their own internal weakness and unfaithfulness. We propose that the churches must now, both in sheer obedience and for their own healing, commit themselves anew to the biblical vision articulated at New Delhi.[64]

That vision included a recovery of concern for the apostolic faith in conjunction with the pursuit of Christian ecumenism, the latter being a necessary context for the recovery of the former.[65]

---

61. Braaten and Jenson, *In One Body Through the Cross*, p. 5.

62. I was an alternate delegate to that gathering, but not present since my church's full delegation was able to attend, yet I followed it with passion. I agree wholeheartedly with the affirmation cited in the study that Christ calls his church to a unity.

63. Braaten and Jenson, *In One Body Through the Cross*, p. 11.

64. Braaten and Jenson, *In One Body Through the Cross*.

65. Making a similar, though more nuanced indictment, and appealing to the same New Delhi vision was veteran ecumenist, Michael Kinnamon, in *The Vision of the Ecumenical Movement and How It Has Been Impoverished by Its Friends* (St. Louis: Chalice Press, 2003). See also the article by Jayson Byassee, "Purpose-Driven Brazil," with its astute evaluation of

The picture of the state of *kerygma* in the mainline churches would not be complete without reference to *counter-evidence* of decline in proclamation of Christian basics, indeed the very showcase of tendencies in cultural captivity to which we have alluded, in the United Church of Christ. Responding to urgings from the Confessing Christ movement for its 2005 General Synod not to settle for voting down a resolution to reclaim traditional Christian teaching (posed in an acerbic fashion by a conservative caucus still in the church but hinting of schism), the delegates approved by a wide margin an alternative resolution reclaiming the church's classical teachings in its founding documents on Jesus Christ as its "sole Head, Son of God and Savior" and the commitment of its six thousand congregations to Christ as "Lord and Savior," and reaffirming as its denominational logo the cross and crown of Christ over the orb of the world. Comparable reclamations are to be found elsewhere, as in the document "Hope in the Lord Jesus Christ" from the Office of Theology and Worship of the Presbyterian Church USA. Is such counter-evidence a sign of an indefatigable Spirit's kerygmatic work among us?

Diakonia

"6:15 PM, time to quit the Lehrer News Program and get on your horse!" says Dorothy. It was "Hospitality Night" at South Church, and I was scheduled to get to the Salvation Army building in a few minutes to pick up five homeless women and drive them to our Fellowship Hall for a warm sleepover on a freezing December night. Two years ago the congregation had joined a coalition of Cape Cod churches formed to provide overnight accommodations for the shocking number of those without hearth or home in what many considered the playground of America's east coast.[66]

Does the outreach to the homeless, replicated many times over elsewhere in the country in projects from soup kitchens to cadres of parishioners wielding hammer and saw for Habitat for Humanity, mean that *diakonia* is

the strengths and weaknesses of the growing Pentecostalism/evangelicalism in that region, but, at the same time, the need for the World Council of Churches, its leaders meeting nearby, to be in dialogue with, and learn from, the dynamisms of that movement. *The Christian Century* 123, no. 7 (April 4, 2006): 8-9.

66. Cape Cod has the highest levels of poverty in the state of Massachusetts.

alive and well in the mainline churches? Surely the evidence is there. But we must ask: Is also to be found here, as in the 1960s, a partner struggle with the social, political, and economic causes of human misery that marked that Day of Diakonia? Is there an equivalent participation in a get-out-the-vote campaign to elect county commissioners who will build housing for the homeless who die on the city streets daily? Are there marches on the state house to demand the prioritizing of poverty on its agenda?

To see who is organizing get-out-the-vote campaigns for their candidates and marching on capitols, state and national — indeed for other kinds of issues — one must turn from the dwindling mainline nation to "the evangelical empire." Now it is not clerical collars, but waving Bibles that occupy the television screen when news is made of religion-in-the-streets. Jerry Falwell told a *New Yorker* essayist some years ago that he had learned from Martin Luther King, Jr., how to make the church's voice of conscience known and effective.[67] While Falwell is no longer the prima donna of the movement, his characterization of political fundamentalism was prescient. The churchly troops mustered to elect presidents, pass legislation, and shape culture are accordingly not those of mainline 1960s markings, but rather the multitudes whose talking heads advocate "moral values" and appear to be, for now at least, in the country's driver's seat. In our categories, these are the present stewards of social and systemic *diakonia*.

With their new visibility comes an interpretation of "moral values" that makes them synonymous with personal virtue, and in functional terms, a "personal" that returns ever and again to its sexual dimensions. A vacuum left by the mainline churches on the personal virtues invites just this kind of attention. Rallies, voting campaigns, demonstrations, civil disobedience — all the tactics of an earlier freedom revolution — now focus on issues of abortion, homosexuality, sexual promiscuity, and pornography. The Religious Right has taken up the earlier activist mainline church's stance in the streets, courts, and halls of government. Indeed, some clerical collars are still visible there, but this time Roman ones (as in "Catholics and evangelicals together"), lockstep on the sanctity of the person from stem cell to fetal beginnings to the marital bed.[68] Will its public diaconal

---

67. Cited in Frances Fitzgerald, "A Disciplined, Charging Army," *The New Yorker,* May 18, 1981, pp. 60-63, 113-14.

68. And to the end of life as well, as in the resistance to anything that hints of euthanasia. For an interesting commentary on this, and the alliance of evangelicals and Roman Catho-

protestations have an equivalent effect on the institutions of American society to that of Martin Luther King, Jr., and his mainline church protagonists? Time will tell.

A simple picture of the displacement of mainline public diaconal witness by that of the presence and successes of the Religious Right, however, will not do. For one, there is the public witness of the African American churches. They gave the lead to the mainline denominations in the era of Martin Luther King, and may yet do it again. To their witness is to be added that of other minority group churches, with issues now expanded to include the fight against the cultures of drugs and crime, and matters of war and work that affect preeminently minority populations.[69]

Back to the mainline. First, some indicators in the fate suffered by highly touted "new forms" of social witness proclaimed by many activists of the 1960s as the real locus of mission. The mainline church coffee house movement is as extinct as Lancaster's Encounter, once the showcase of congregational efforts to reach out into "the world."[70] So too, other para-congregational ventures announced as harbingers of needed "new forms" have suffered the same fate, among them the industrial mission, metropolitan missioner, shopping mall and leisure center mission, and "ministry of presence" experiments.[71] The institutionalization of social concern by their location in a "center" that was linked to a cathedral church and an educational center in the expected reconfiguration caused by secularization and ecumenism never did happen, and its theories are now long gone.[72]

Yet there are ironies. The voice of the mainline does continue to be

---

lics, see Richard Neuhaus's response to commentary on the twentieth anniversary of his prescient *The Naked Public Square*, "Richard John Neuhaus," *First Things* 147 (November 2004): 24-26.

69. So the African American congregations and pastors that led that struggle in our own Boston environs, reflecting a national pattern.

70. Encounter, after a vigorous decade of involvements in the issues of "being, having, and belonging" including the helping into being and hosting of a citizens' newspaper, the *Lancaster Independent Press* — giving the establishment "some LIP" — as it was said, went out of existence in the 1970s, and the paper, leaving behind more and more its ecclesial roots, went out of business in the 1980s. See Gabriel Fackre, "A Voice for the Voiceless," *Journal* 7, no. 11 (September 1969): 3-7.

71. Gabriel Fackre, "Ministry as Presence," in *Dictionary of Pastoral Care*, ed. R. Hunter (Nashville: Abingdon Press, 1990), pp. 950-51.

72. See the author's hopeful "COCU from the Ground Up," *Andover Newton Quarterly* 12, no. 1 (September 1971): 34-41.

heard in the public square. However, it is often less on the defining 1960s issues of "being, having, and belonging" and more on the same culture-war issues of personal morality given pride of place by the Religious Right, but a voice at different vocal levels and with mixed messages. Often the mainline churches' bureaucracies speak loud and clear on the other side of personal moral questions — pro-choice vs. pro-life on abortion, pro same-gender vs. pro-family, pro-free speech vs. anti-pornography. At the same time, there often appears tacit and sometimes vocal support for the "moral values" constituency's position on fetal dignity and marriage, and shock over the culture of pornography among grassroots people and pastors in mainline congregations.[73]

The national voice of mainline churches does continue to be heard on 1960s-like issues of social justice, notably matters of war and peace. A denominational officer may be found, on occasion, on a picket line or even under arrest. Yet the impact of such phenomena bears no comparison to the presence and influence of leaders, pastors, and members in the freedom revolution of an earlier decade. And no comparison, either, to the visibility and influence of the Religious Right in the public square.

Adding to the ironies and the complexities of the picture of *diakonia* in the present context is the capacity of those in Roman collars to make an effective witness on issues of personal morality. The exposure of the extent of pedophilia and ephebophelia in the ranks of Roman Catholic clergy weakens the most carefully honed and passionate doctrinal arguments for the personal virtues. The picture of priests in the courtroom in 2004 charged with sexual molestation is quite different from priests in the courtroom in 1964 charged with pouring blood on FBI files, or again, priests being driven out of their churches today by the testimony of altar boys compared to priests marching in another decade against racial oppression. The same weakening is evident in important and needed Roman Catholic public commentary on issues of war and peace, as well as matters of personal morality.

Again, too-simple either-or taxonomies — mainline vs. evangelical —

73. So too this mainliner who joined with others in the liberal UCC to speak a word for "marriage in the Christian tradition" in response to the Massachusetts Supreme Judicial Court's 4-3 endorsement of same-gender marriage. See the Internet website, uccmarriagediscussion.com. On the abortion issue, see the essay by writer and spouse, "Abortion," in James W. Cox, ed., *Handbook of Themes for Preaching* (Louisville: Westminster/John Knox Press, 1991), pp. 23-27.

do not account for significant phalanxes among the evangelical troops that do not march to the drumbeat of the Religious Right. There is a cadre of "justice and peace evangelicals"[74] who, while strongly advocating "moral values" in their personal dimension, also press for an enlargement of the concept to include the public issues of peace, poverty, and race, and do so with some effectiveness.[75] Again, ironically these evangelical are the heirs and most vocal representatives of the "being, having, and belonging" agenda of the mainline church of the 1960s. On the same matter of complexity, the Religious Right has its own take on those issues as well as its foreground focus on personal morality, giving vigorous support to national war policy and patriotism, and in a time of war influencing and advancing an administration so identified. The shifts, ironies, and complexities in ecclesial *diakonia*, public and personal, are the setting in which we find ourselves as we ask what this sign of the Holy Spirit means for the church in the opening years of a new century and millennium.[76]

74. "Evangelical, Evangelicalism," in Alan Richardson and John Bowden, eds., *Westminster Dictionary of Christian Theology*, revised edition (Philadelphia: Westminster Press, 1983), pp. 190-91.

75. So the regular representation in the media of that group by Jim Wallis, editor of the journal *Sojourners*, a principal megaphone for justice and peace evangelicals. A high point in its public witness at a critical election period when "evangelical" came to be associated in many public venues with the Religious Right was its full-page ad several days before the 2004 national election linking the anniversary of the Barmen Declaration of 1934 with a protest against then-current war-making by the administration, "Confessing Christ in an Age of Violence." See also his *God's Politics: Why the Right Gets It Wrong and the Left Doesn't Get It* (New York: HarperCollins, 2005).

76. Not mentioned in the foregoing account are those for whom "doing" comes in yet other forms. The phenomenon of the megachurch does not sit easily in any of the aforementioned categories. The size and diversity of its congregations and broad appeal do not square with narrow political agendas or partisan politics. For all that, *diakonia* in one form constitutes its central appeal. That is the congregation, especially so in its small groups, but also its general style in leadership, worship practice, preaching, and general programming that give pride of place to the "therapeutic." Here healing can be found for the anxious spirit, the troubled marriage, the dysfunctional family, the frustrations of the workplace, and the uncertainties of the times. The church is the environment for the caring deeds to be done, not the world outside its doors. The earlier reference to the world-scale ministry of Rick Warren and his Saddleback congregation may signal a new turn outwards in the megachurches. Time will tell.

Leitourgia

What happens today when a congregation decides it needs a new hymnbook? Such a moment is a showcase of the state of worship, broadly characterized here as *leitourgia*. We focus on one congregation again, and the dynamics fore and aft, of the selection and reception process.

A loyal pastor in the 1970s had convinced South Church, Centerville, Massachusetts, to place in its pew racks the new *United Church of Christ Hymnal*. The hymnody was classical but also included contemporary music that came out of the civil rights movement that was current during its preparation. Within its covers were the then-new UCC eucharistic liturgies, chants, responses, readings, psalmody, the church-year lections, and the ancient creeds, all of it designed by a Hymnal Committee significantly influenced by the liturgical renewal within ecumenism. Also, with its attunement to both UCC identity and theological substance, its structure was based on the sequence of affirmations in the UCC Statement of Faith.

This hymnal was a staple of the congregation for a quarter of a century, and the piety of the people was shaped by it accordingly. Hymnbooks do deteriorate and times do change. Also, complaints had been lodged by some in the choir and the congregation that the selection in the present hymnal was too limited, and more recent pastors and interim ministers had been printing other hymns in the Sunday bulletins to supplement this list. In the 1990s, an instrumentality of the denomination produced *The New Century Hymnal,* the result of the request of an earlier General Synod of the Church to provide a new hymnal the language of which would be both more contemporary and more inclusive. The latter was related to "inclusive language" issues such as the elimination of any terms that excluded women and carried forth the patriarchy seen to infect both the theology and terminology of the church. Inclusivity also meant the widening of the voices in a hymnbook to include ethnic traditions previously marginalized or ignored. This "new hymnbook" talk in the denomination was also in the air as South Church considered its own choices.

Within the congregation were voices that strongly opposed *The New Century Hymnal* on the grounds that the well-intentioned effort at inclusivity eventuated in careless re-translation of standard hymns, altering their theology, and the frequent removal of terms such as "Lord," "Father," and "Son of God," which were integral to Christian teaching and ecumenical faith, with meanings that were not taken from patriarchy but in fact challenged it.[77] There was little desire to go that way in the selection committee, but what were the alternatives? Could some recognition of the need for inclusivity be combined with the larger range of hymnody desired? As the inclusive-language hymnals that did not eliminate key Christian language, and also had a rich range of music currently available, were published by denominations other than that of the congregation,[78] perhaps a hymnal by a non-denominational publisher would be the better choice? After a general airing of this view, with some heated opposition, the congregation endorsed the committee's proposal for the purchase of the Hope Publishing Company's *Worship and Rejoice* hymnal.

With an eye on a potential audience for the then-growing "praise music," the hymnal producers had added to this version many songs in that genre. Such proved to be an entry point at South Church for the "worship wars." The language reflects that of the "culture wars," and indeed, the battle imagery is appropriate in the former as it has been in the latter. In both cases the unity of the church sought and threatened in the present state of *koinonia* appears again in *leitourgia* as it did in *diakonia*. But the illustration of it in South Church is not only the conventional reading of the struggle as between evangelical praise music and ecumenical classics. The dispute, when placed in the longer context of inclusive language, evidences a deeper polarity and some more intriguing ironies. On the one hand is a new surge of pietism that presses for ways of worship that satisfy its experiential needs, and on the other, a religious activism that requires worship to conform to its own experiential interests. While the division is deep, the irony is that both are beholden to the norm of "experience" in matters of *leitourgia*. The "I, me, and mine" refrains in contemporary praise music have their counterpart in the postmodern "it works for me" worship that conforms to the current standards of political correctness. In jeopardy are the biblical and classical standards of the liturgical renewal movement and the convergence represented in its better days.

---

77. For this critique, see Richard Christensen, ed., *How Shall We Sing the Lord's Song? An Assessment of the New Century Hymnal* (Allison Park, Pa.: Pickwick Publications, 1997). The writer's contributions were "UCC Theological Basics: An Interpretation," and "Hymn Texts and Key Christian Teachings."

78. So the writer's survey, "Christian Teaching and Inclusive Language Hymnody," *The Hymn* 50, no. 2 (April 1999): 26-32. For an excellent study of this subject and how "praise music" can be reoriented to "orthodox doxology," see Frank C. Sen, "The Challenge of Pentecostal Praise and Orthodox Doxology," *Lutheran Forum* 39, no. 3 (Fall 2005): 16-24.

While currently only on the horizon of today's state of *leitourgia,* another issue will come further to the fore in the years ahead, that of the "open Table." As practice here and there in congregations of various mainline denominations, to invite "all" to the Table means *all.* The eucharist is not a "Meal" for those who have had a "Bath," but rather a Table set for any who choose to come, including the unbaptized, those of other faiths or of no faith. Why so? Answer: that kind of hospitality is the same as the indiscriminate welcome of Jesus. What else is Christianity if it is not "extravagant" love?[79]

We shall take up the relation of baptism to eucharist in the chapter on the liturgical marks of the church. For now, it's worth mentioning how this construal of an "open table" is a departure from the doctrine and practice of the historic church with its nexus between the two sacraments, as in the recent convergence document, *BEM,* a creature of the *leitourgia* decade earlier reviewed, as well as ecumenical statements and the eucharistic teaching of historic Christian churches. Here, yet again, is another life apart that marks the twenty-first-century mainline churches, one accompanied by the same irony earlier mentioned: a convergence based upon the normativity of experience, secular or pious, over biblical and classical teaching on an aspect of the doctrine of the church.

*   *   *

This investigation of the doctrine of the church has begun with two acts of discernment, and two narratives. The source of ecclesiology is Scripture, here understood in terms of the Acts account of the signs of the Spirit, as illumined by the New Testament's trinitarian and christological images. This Christian teaching, as all others, is interpreted, ever and again, in the historical setting to which it speaks. Hence our second act of discernment and narrative had to do with the state of the church as lived out in local and at-large contexts in the run-up to the present as it is now perceived to be in the mainline churches served by today's pastors.

How then are the signs in both narratives to be related to the standard topics of ecclesiology? In the next and final chapter of Part I, their interrelationship will be addressed. In Part II, a deeper exploration of each sign, attribute, mark, and model will be undertaken.

79. On this subject, see the writer's article "The 'Open Table' in Mercersburg Perspective," *The New Mercersburg Review* 37 (Fall 2006).

CHAPTER 3

Signs, Attributes, Marks, and Models

What then is the relation of "the signs of the Spirit" manifest in the primitive church and discerned in a fragmentary and ambiguous way in the life of the church in recent decades and in the present, to the traditional "attributes" and "marks" of the church? And to the models and images of more current analysis? To that we now turn in preparation for an examination of each sign/attribute/mark/model, and to their divine-human nature pointed to in our images of the church. As will be seen, the correlation seeks to illumine several yet-to-be-explored aspects of the historic attributes.

Koinonia and Its Companions

Koinonia as it came to be in the pentecostal community was a *life together,* a "fellowship" of the Spirit that mirrored the Life Together of the triune God. This people of God had a being "in common," a radical *caring* that reflected — albeit in human terms, ones soon to be seen in other New Testament accounts, as marred by sin and limited by finitude — the unity in diversity of the divine Being Together. As such, this communion of saints was a portent of the eschatological "being together" for which a redeemed creation is destined.

In recent ecumenical self-understandings and outreach, *communio* has been a foreground figure for churches in quest of a larger unity. The concept of "communion" to which the Latin word points is identical with *koinonia* as a sign of the Holy Spirit. *Koinonia/communio*/communion — a convergence of ways of expressing *unity* as a defining attribute of the church. In all cases, as in the divine Life Together, unity does not mean uniformity, a collapse of the differences into monolithicity. Rather, as in Paul's Corinthian vision, the charisms are joined in a mutuality that builds up the Body of Christ. Of such is a unity that testifies to the diversity and mutuality of the Persons of the Trinity, the latter, albeit with a coinherence known only in deity.

It is no accident that the model of the church as "mystical communion" is described by Avery Dulles in similar terms. Drawing on Dietrich Bonhoeffer's characterization of such in his work, *The Communion of Saints,* this model is one in which "the community is constituted by the complete self-forgetfulness of love. The relationship between I and Thou is no longer a demanding but a giving one."[1] What else is this than a mirror of the divine Life Together and thus a sign of the Spirit's gift of *koinonia* and manifestation of the attribute of unity intended for the mystical Body of Christ on earth?

As with all the traditional attributes, we must ask: What of the claims of being "church" where there is no such visible sign? Can there be unity, an attribute indispensable to being church, where there is division instead?

The church universal today is awash in division. The same could be said for a given denomination. And the partisanships descend to the base ecclesial communities, local congregations. The toll taken by such a breach of Christ's purposes for his Body is inestimable. Where there is division,

---

1. Avery Dulles, *Models of the Church* (New York: Doubleday, 1978), p. 44. Bonhoeffer's work *Life Together* returns to this theme, the language of the title giving us the terms used throughout this volume. See *Life Together,* trans. with Introduction by John W. Doberstein (New York: Harper & Bros., 1954). How deep the meaning of this phrase was to Bonhoeffer can be seen vividly in Eberhard Bethge's biography of Bonhoeffer, especially in the years 1936-37 when the Confessing Church, its pastors, and Bonhoeffer's Finkenwalde seminary students, were under heavy attack with many arrests made by the Nazi government. The importance of bonding included the risky announcement in church of the names of those in prison as well as prayers for them, acts forbidden by the state with attendant punishment. See Eberhard Bethge, *Dietrich Bonhoeffer: A Biography,* rev. and ed. Victorial J. Barnett (Minneapolis: Fortress Press, 2000), pp. 561-86 and *passim.*

the church universal and every derivative expression are under judgment. Stern warnings of such are heard in the New Testament.

Indeed, the first encounter with ecclesial strife occurs at the church's very beginnings. To the fractious Corinthians, Paul says,

> I appeal to you, brothers and sisters, by the name of Jesus Christ, that all of you be in agreement and that there be no divisions among you, but that you be united. . . . (1 Cor. 1:10)

Riddled with controversies among the parties of Paul, Apollos, Cephas, and even the party of "Christ," the early Christian divisions were a portent of the fissiparous tendencies that continue to this day. So shorn of the indispensable attribute of unity, does the church then cease to be? Paul did not say that to the Corinthian congregation. Rather he began his letter:

> To the church of God that is in Corinth, to those who are sanctified in Christ Jesus. . . . (1 Cor. 1:2)

And again, in the midst of another rebuke of those at Corinth who, like the eye or the foot in a body that says to other parts, "I have no need of you," Paul declares:

> Now you are the body of Christ and individually members of it. (1 Cor. 12:27)

This must mean, if unity is an indispensable attribute of the church, that it still exists, in some sense, even in a divided church. How that is the case will be a matter high on our ecclesiological agenda. At this point, we can say, it has to do with the church as a divine-human organism, a whole Body of Christ *coram Deo*, even though it be a broken Body of Christ *coram humanitas*, with a sign of the Spirit seen only by the eye of God, while withheld from our sight, although not without the promise of the possibilities of historical embodiment. This point will be developed briefly in connection with the section here on *diakonia* and in greater detail in Part II.

Diakonia and Its Companions

Diakonia as it came to be in the pentecostal church had to do with a radical *sharing* intermixed with the radical *caring* of its life together. The things they had in common were the bread of earth that sustained daily life as well as the "bread of heaven" in the Lord's Supper. Bodies counted, as well as souls: those of society's rejected widows, women, orphans, slaves, prisoners, poor, infants destined for a merciless exposure to the elements and left to wither and die. Bodies were for healing as well, by whatever means at hand, by medication bought with "silver and gold," and when there was none by a work of the Spirit, extraordinary as well as ordinary (Acts 3:6). All this kind of physical caring and sharing had to do with the Holy Spirit's sign of serving, *diakonia*. And, as such, it mirrored the giving and serving of the Persons, one to another in the God without a body, but who with the same divine *diakonia* came among us, incarnate in the Word made flesh of one who went about healing bodies, and calling for binding up wounds by human hands.

Serving the neighbor in rudimentary need is a holy act, understanding holiness here in its horizontal sense as the life of Christian *agape*. Of course, "holiness" and "the holy" bespeak as well a verticality, "the sacred," the things of the holy God and the life of piety associated therewith. We shall explore the relation of the holiness of the church in the latter sense to the former meaning in Part II, with some indications of the relation in the following. Here, in the earliest narrative of the church, it is the actual manifestation of holiness as *diakonia* that gives us a framework for understanding the classical ecclesial attribute "sanctity," relating it to that sign of the Holy Spirit. The church is the community where are to be found the "acts," not just the talks, of the apostles, where they "walk the walk as well as talk the talk." By this measure, the church is known by its fruits (Matt. 7:16) and may be found where there is the outreach to the last and the least in their most elementary Samaritan road needs.

Another of the Dulles models gives pride of place to *diakonia*, "the church as servant." Representative for him is a 1966 pastoral letter of Cardinal Cushing of Boston (a letter reflecting the diaconal emphasis of the decade):

> So it is that the Church announces the coming of the Kingdom not only in word, through preaching and proclamation, but more particularly in work, in her ministry of reconciliation, of binding up wounds, of suffering service, of healing. . . . And the Lord was the "man for others." So must the Church be "the community for others."[2]

2. Dulles, *Models of the Church*, p. 86. Interestingly, the cardinal draws on the image of

As with the other models, Dulles finds troubling the reduction of the church to this single emphasis on service, but, as in his approval of Cardinal Cushing's version of it, sees its emphasis on *diakonia* as integral to any full understanding of the nature of the church.

As with the first attribute, we must ask again: Does the absence of the evidence of a serving holiness thereby dissolve the reality of the church? Not a few defenders of "the church for others" in the 1960s believed that to be the case, as noted. No "participation in the sufferings of God in the world" (again, the Bonhoeffer background), then no legitimate claim to be the church, hence the call to turn from the local congregation to secular mission and its "new forms." Yet, does the practice of even the most passionate good works exhaust the ecclesial attribute of holiness?

The holiness of the church does not stand or fall with diaconal deeds, any more than does the justification of the sinner depend on good works. The church's attribute of holiness, as is the case with others, is bidimensional, divine as well as human. As the church is one in the eyes of God, in spite of its division, so the church is holy in the divine sight, even in its tawdry record of servanthood. Its ontological holiness resides in the presence of the Spirit as promised by the Son, and that to the very end of the Story (Matt. 28:20), regardless of our diaconal waywardness. So, again Paul can speak to the very ones he berates in the words cited earlier; he can address the wayward as "those who are sanctified in Christ Jesus" (1 Cor. 1:2). The church's holiness, as a sign seen only by its Lord, resides in his presence among us, a grace abounding to sinners.

Yet, more is to be said. Are those who are "sanctified in Christ Jesus" only so in principle, not also in fact? As there is no justification of the sinner without the promises of sanctification, how can there be a church without the same promise? Where there is pardon there is the promise of power — in the church as in the believer. The giving of the visible sign of *diakonia* to the expression of church is proof of the promise. While at a given point in time, the evidence of such may not be for our eyes to see, the work of the Spirit will not be defeated.

The sign of power may appear in unexpected ways. As with the failures in unity, so too the abdication of the pursuit of holiness carries with it a cost. Such a church stands under judgment, and a price will be paid for its

---

Dietrich Bonhoeffer — "the man for others" — so influential in that era, not only on the attribute of unity, but also sanctity.

unfruitfulness. So the account of these things in Acts makes clear about an elemental breach in stewardship of things material necessary for the care of bodies. To Ananias and Sapphira who conspired to hold back monies needed for the servant church came the words:

> "How is it that you have contrived this deed in your heart? You did not lie to us but to God!" (Acts 5:4)

And the consequences were deadly for the two deceivers. The pentecostal congregation did not cease to be because of the avarice of its members, but was put on notice and suffered in the limbs of its body. A fair warning to a church remiss in its diaconal duty.[3]

But the promise is, finally, of sanctifying power, the coming to be of deeds of *diakonia*. If not here, then there. If not now, therefore, then. To be continued when we explore in detail the signs of the Holy Spirit.

A question latent in all the foregoing: What then assures us that any empirical body of people is also the Body of Christ if two of its visible signs are missing, or difficult to discern — unity and sanctity? For an answer we turn to the final two attributes, and why they came to the fore in the Reformation, and were spoken of as the defining "marks of the church."

Leitourgia and Its Companions

Thousands baptized, much bread broken, many prayers said. The worship of God in its varied ways was integral to being the primitive people of God. Here was the heart of the community beating by the power of the Holy Spirit even as its praise and prayer were lifted to the Father in the name of the Son. This verticality was descent as well as ascent, for water, bread, wine, and prayer were the means of grace that brought the Body to be and nurtured it with the food of heaven. This worship was "the work of the people," to and through the presence and power of the triune God — *leitourgia*.

The liturgical life of the people of God was then, and is now, a very spe-

---

3. A note struck in the 1960s debate on these matters. See "The Crisis of the Congregation," *Voluntary Associations: A Study of Groups in Free Societies*. Essays in Honor of James Luther Adams, ed. D. B. Robertson (Richmond, Va.: John Knox Press, 1966).

cial sign of the Spirit. It is the attribute whose appearance assures the *catholicity* of the gathering that claims to be "church." Where the baptized assemble for the bread and the wine, over which prayers are offered and in conjunction with which the Word is proclaimed, we have to do with *eucharist*. Wherever those bathed in baptism gather in prayer for the Meal, there the church catholic is present.

Catholicity, of course, is "universality." Over time, the theology of the church has sought to say what that means. Universality is the church in every geographic place? In every time? Pointed therein or purposed as such? So conceived, it is difficult for any one claimant to define itself as requiring these conditions, every nook and cranny of space or time being not so accessible, and the pointing and purposing not so discernible. Some more fundamental meaning must attach to catholicity.

If the pentecostal church is our paradigm, then surely it was catholic/universal. How so geographically, or spread over the ages, when it inhabited such a scandalously particular place and time? Rather, its catholicity consisted in its celebrations surrounding the entrance of those by water into a community that gathered about a table to meet ever and again their Lord in the breaking of the bread and hearing of the Word.[4] As then, so now, where there is eucharist, there is catholicity. The attribute of universality is constituted by the celebration of the Lord's Supper including the preached Word. Where that happens the universal Lord grants that assembly catholicity. In a powerful argument from within Eastern Orthodox premises, Fr. Paul Wesche rightly reminds us of the patristic roots of this conviction: "The criterion of catholic orthodoxy for St. Ignatius is the *eucharist*. . . ."[5]

Avery Dulles's description of the model of "the church as sacrament" echoes the foregoing:

> The Eucharist is individually Christological and ecclesiological. In its Christological aspect it actualizes in a palpable way the presence of the Redeemer with the congregation of those who look to him in love and

---

4. Eucharist so understood is never without the preached Word, as in the definition of the ecumenical text, *Baptism, Eucharist and Ministry* (Geneva: World Council of Churches, 1982), pp. 10, 15.

5. So the section "Marks of Catholicity" in his "The Eucharist as Criterion of Orthodoxy," in Carl E. Braaten and Robert W. Jenson, eds., *Marks of the Body of Christ* (Grand Rapids: Eerdmans, 1999), pp. 75-80.

trust. In its ecclesiological aspect the Eucharist celebrates and solidi-
fies the union of the faithful with one another about the holy table.[6]

Following his Roman Catholic understanding of the nature of the
church, Cardinal Dulles would require a right ordering of the ministry, one
in apostolic succession, for the full validity of such a eucharist.[7] However, it
is interesting to note the view of the conjunction of eucharist with that of a
catholicity not so confined to special church order in these observations of
Fr. George Tavard on the intention of the Second Vatican Council:

> Where it finds the Eucharist, it finds the church. . . . [T]he Reforma-
> tion focussed attention on two marks, notes or signs, of the church:
> "where the Word is preached and the sacraments are administered
> according to the gospel." This was in fact an amplification of the defi-
> nition of the church by Thomas Aquinas: The church is the gathering
> of the faithful *(congregatio fidelium)*. Aquinas and medieval theology
> in general did not define the church by the hierarchy or *magisterium*.
> This is a later point of view, typical of the counter-Reformation. . . .
> Defining the church by the faithful, implicitly raises the question of
> what makes the faithful faithful? They are faithful because they have
> heard the Word of God in the Holy Spirit, and they have been led by
> it to Christ, present among us in the Eucharist. . . . The fundamental
> ecclesiology is that the church is the communion of the faithful,
> gathered in Christ through the Holy Spirit.[8]

In a similar vein Susan Wood comments,

> There is a density of ontological realism here that extends not only to
> the sacramental realism of the presence of Christ under the species of
> bread and wine, but also a sacramental realism of the church, for
> where the Eucharist is, there is the church. There is an intrinsic rela-

---

6. Dulles, *Models of the Church*, p. 65.

7. The same would be true of Eastern Orthodoxy, regarding the validity of the eucharist
as inseparable from a priest ordained by a bishop in apostolic succession, although not ordered by a papacy. See John Meyendorff, *Catholicity and the Church* (Crestwood, N.Y.: St.
Vladimir's Seminary Press, 1983), pp. 26-29, 59-64, and *passim*.

8. George Tavard, "Ecumenical Perspectives on the Leuenberg Agreement," in *The
Leuenberg Agreement and Lutheran-Reformed Relationships*, ed. William Rusch and Daniel F.
Martensen (Minneapolis: Augsburg Press, 1989), pp. 121, 122.

tionship between the historical Christ, the sacramental Christ and the ecclesial Christ.[9]

The implication of this interpretation of the church's fundamental reality by Roman Catholic theologians as centered in the eucharist is that catholicity resides in the celebration, binding together each in all places who so meet Jesus Christ. How the *well-being* of the church, or its well-being in terms of the ordering of its ministry, is related to this, is another and quite important matter. The point here is that the church's catholic being, so understood, inheres in its eucharistic practice.[10]

With this "high" view of the eucharist, we are approaching, as indicated by Fr. Tavard's remarks, the reason the Reformation spoke, primarily, of two *notae ecclesiae*.[11] These "marks" of the church were: the faithful preaching of the gospel and right administration of the sacraments.[12] Where they happened the church was deemed to exist.[13] When the eucharist is understood, as in the *BEM* convergence document, as the sacrament of the Lord's Supper which, of necessity, includes the preaching of the gospel, then both marks are present in the one core practice of the church.

What then of the other two, whether described as the signs of *koinonia* and *diakonia* or as the attributes of unity and sanctity? We have anticipated the answer to that in the New Testament assertion of the being of the church, even when the attributes and visible signs of unity and holiness

9. "*Communio* Ecclesiology: Source of Hope, Source of Controversy," *Pro Ecclesia* 2, no. 4 (Fall 1993): 425.

10. It should be noted that Pope Benedict XVI while Cardinal held a similar view but made it clear that "The unity among themselves, of the communities that celebrate the Eucharist, is not an external accessory for eucharistic ecclesiology but its inmost condition. . . . It is Catholic, or it does not exist at all." Quoted by Miroslav Volf in *After Our Likeness: The Church as the Image of the Trinity* (Grand Rapids: Eerdmans, 1998), pp. 44, 45.

11. Others were added in some quarters, as for example "church discipline" in the Reformed tradition. Luther, in *On the Councils and the Church*, lengthened the list to include "the office of the keys, or church discipline; ordained ministry; prayer, doxology, catechesis; and the way of the cross or discipleship," so described by Reinhard Hütter in *Bound to Be Free: Evangelical Catholic Engagements in Ecclesiology, Ethics, and Ecumenism* (Grand Rapids: Eerdmans, 2004), a volume and point of view to which we shall return.

12. As in Mark A. Noll, ed., *Confessions and Catechisms of the Reformation* (Grand Rapids: Baker, 1991) and Arthur C. Cochrane, ed. With historical Introductions, New Introduction by Jack Rogers (Philadelphia: Westminster/John Knox, 2003).

13. See Gordon W. Lathrop and Timothy J. Wengert, *Christian Assembly: Marks of the Church in a Pluralist Age* (Minneapolis: Fortress Press, 2004), *passim*.

were missing at a point in time, or ambiguous. We pursue it further in taking up the final sign of the Spirit in the church.

Kerygma and Its Companions

"But Peter, standing with the eleven, raised his voice and addressed them . . ." (Acts 2:14). So came the first *kerygma* in the Christian church's history, the proclamation of the Word. And what was the Word? It was the gospel story, the good news of "Jesus of Nazareth" with its origins in the plan of the Father, its outworking in the election of Isrel, its prophets pointing to the coming One who lived, taught, was crucified, and rose again, the Spirit's outpouring here and now, the call to repentance and a new life together with God and one another, the promise of even greater things to come (Acts 2:14-40).

When a later church had to speak its Word, nurturing a new generation in the faith, distinguishing true from false teaching, it returned to the Story, putting it into a baptismal profession that went from creation to consummation with its center-point in Jesus Christ. That credo took on a life of its own in second-century Christianity, its affirmations honored as the testimony of those first to tell the Story, and thus an "apostles'" creed, a "rule of faith" for believers, but also a standard for defenders of the faith to expound in the back-and-forth with the church's antagonists. Thus where lips professed this creed, told this Story, proclaimed this Word, there existed the true church of the apostles, constituted so by this the kerygmatic sign of *apostolicity.* As such, of course, the preached and taught Good News could only come from texts with *like* authority, hence "*apostolic* writings" soon to be more formally assembled and designated along with the book of the Hebrew people as sacred Scripture. Are there privileged interpreters of creed and Scripture, those whose lineage is in continuity with the pentecostal leaders, and thus an "*apostolic* ministry"? To be continued. Here we associate the attribute of apostolicity with the Petrine gift of the kerygmatic Word, continuity with which is decisive for the being of the church.

The Dulles model that gives pride of place to the proclaimed Word is "the church as herald":

This model is kerygmatic, for it looks upon the Church as a herald — one who receives an official message with the commission to pass it on. The basic image is that of the herald of a king, who comes to proclaim a royal decree in a public square.[14]

"Word and Sacrament" — the hallmarks of the church and the means of grace in the Reformation traditions — are the tests of where unity, holiness, catholicity, and apostolicity are to be found. Stated otherwise, in the light of our sequencing, the last two signs of the Spirit, as visible to our eyes and hearable by our ears, are not only empirical manifestations of the ontological realities *coram Deo,* but are also the guarantee that the seeming absence *empirically* of evidence of unity and sanctity does not preclude the presence of these same attributes *ontologically.* Thus when we see a church divided, lacking *koinonia,* and call for the hidden ontological unity to be made manifest, the justification for that mandate and hope is the surety that the church of discord is, before God, a true church of unity albeit *invisible* to our eyes and awaiting realization in time and space, made such by the *visible* marks of Word and Sacrament in which Christ, the second Person of the triune God, is truly present. And likewise, when we see an unholy empirical church, lacking in *diakonia,* and assert its holiness, we do so because we believe it is, before God, holy, and therefore properly called to make, and promised to have, visible that attribute, because it enjoys the marks of the church, Word and Sacrament, in which Christ, the second Person of the triune God, is truly present. The eucharist, which joins the preached word to the celebrated sacraments in their catholic unity, is therefore where the church always and everywhere is. Put in another way, the marks of the church are "objective" and as such, do not stand or fall with the performance of "subjective" good works or the behavior of unity and sanctity. What does stand or fall, as a communion rite puts it regarding faithful reception, is whether the objective marks of the church are "unto damnation" or "unto salvation." How they come — to heal or to hurt — depends on whether the marks are welcomed in grace or traduced by human sin. The love of Christ in Word and Sacrament is tough as well as tender.

And tender as well as tough. Grace heals as well as hurts. In the life of the Christian, justification is both forensic — pardon for the sinner received by faith alone, and fructifying — power in the sinner, bearing the fruits of the Spirit in sanctifying love. The same is so for the church, chosen and loved by Christ in spite of its performance, not because of it. Yet, as

14. Dulles, *Models of the Church,* p. 71.

in the believer, so in the Body, grace is power as well as pardon. The Holy Spirit gives signs of that love and the presence of that Head from apostolic days forward. If not immediately discernible at a given point in time — in believer or Body — the promise is made that the invisible shall be made visible. Because of the ontological *invisibility* of the church's true unity and sanctity where there is faithful Word and Sacrament — apostolicity and catholicity — the *visible* fruits of the Spirit will not be denied to the church of Jesus Christ. The Body will yet show signs of healing; the Temple will not remain in ruins; the People will walk in the ways of God.

Because so much depends on the promises of Christ attached to the attributes of apostolicity and catholicity as they are here understood — the faithful preaching of the Word and the right administration of the sacraments — they emerged in the sixteenth-century Reformation as the distinguishing "marks of the church." And they remain so today.[15]

Some will ask: What of those Christian bodies that do *not* have these marks? For example, the Society of Friends and the Salvation Army? Can these that do not share in the foundational marks of proclaimed Word and celebrated Sacrament still be part of the one, holy, catholic, and apostolic church?

From time to time in the history of Christian thought, the logic of what appears to be an uncontestable assertion about the ways of God runs into a piece of counter-evidence that does not fit even the longest and widest consensus in Christian teaching. Is this a reminder to the church of the finitude of its best wisdom? Of the freedom of God that will not be bound by our decree of what must be the case? Of sound doctrinal rules that, nevertheless, do have an exception? Of an eschatological proviso that must acknowledge that our best sight of revelatory light is still only through a glass darkly?

A case can be made that even the rigorous Roman Catholic Church, associating baptism with entry into the one, holy, catholic, and apostolic church, can yet expand its form beyond water and the Word to baptism by martyrdom and baptism by intention when the standard means are not

---

15. For another emphasis on the importance of relating the four classical attributes to the two Reformation marks, see Karl Barth's 1927 lecture "The Concept of the Church" (in Karl Barth, *Theology and Church* [London: SCM Press, 1962]), done in an early period of his dialogue with Roman Catholic theology, a fact noted by Reinhard Hütter in *Bound to Be Free*, pp. 244-45. Barth returns to the interrelationship in 1935 in his work on the Apostles' Creed, *Credo*, English translation with Foreword by Robert McAfee Brown (New York: Charles Scribner's Sons, 1962), pp. 136-49.

accessible. Conciliar Christianity, arguably less demanding in its standards, but not without them, includes the Society of Friends and the Salvation Army in its circles, insofar as its bodies profess some Christian credo. (Perhaps also their good works, too often putting to shame more orthodox denominations, combined with confession of the Word, suggests the same kind of reinterpreted sacramentality as found in the exception granted by the Roman community.) Without qualifying any of the foregoing regarding the cruciality of eucharistic signs of Word and Sacrament for the church's being, let there also be humility before the facts of the divine freedom, our human finitude, and the last Word of the age to come.

By showing the interrelationship of ways of identifying the church in Scripture and tradition, we have arrived at a working definition of our subject. The church is the community of finite and fallen sinners called to be the Body of Christ marked by the faithful proclamation of the Word and celebration of the sacraments, promised the signs of the Holy Spirit in the mission to bring the world to know and participate in the Story of God through its *kerygma, leitourgia, diakonia, and koinonia,* and accorded thereby the attributes of apostolicity, catholicity, sanctity, and unity. It remains for us to examine in depth each of these signs, marks, and attributes of a community human as well as divine, a people finite and frail, yet a People of God, a temple too ready to totter but yet a Temple of the Spirit, a body wounded by sin but yet the Body of Christ.

For Further Reading

For a sampling of other understandings of the attributes/marks/signs/models in the surge in systematic theology (from "primers" to a fourteen-volume series) that began in the late twentieth century, see their treatment in selected passages from these works:

Hendrikus Berkhof, *Christian Faith: An Introduction to the Study of Faith,* revised edition, trans. Sierd Woudstra (Grand Rapids: Eerdmans, 1986), pp. 414-24.

Donald Bloesch, *The Church: Sacraments, Ministry, Mission,* Christian Foundations series (Downers Grove, Ill.: InterVarsity Press, 2002), pp. 99-115.

Philip J. Hefner, "The Being of the Church," in Carl E. Braaten and Robert

Jenson, eds., *Christian Dogmatics*, vol. 2 (Philadelphia: Fortress Press, 1984), pp. 203-21.

Susan Brooks Thistlethwaite and Peter Crafts Hodgson, "The Church, Classism and Ecclesial Community," in Rebecca S. Chopp and Mark Lewis Taylor, eds., *Reconstructing Christian Theology* (Minneapolis: Fortress Press, 1994), pp. 316-25.

James H. Cone, *Liberation: A Black Theology of Liberation* (Philadelphia: J. B. Lippincott, 1970), pp. 228-38.

Michael A. Fahey, "The Nature of the Church in Modern Roman Catholic Teaching," in Francis Schussler Fiorenza and John P. Galvin, eds., *Systematic Theology: Roman Catholic Perspectives*, vol. 2 (Minneapolis: Fortress Press, 1991), pp. 30-43.

Thomas N. Finger, *A Contemporary Anabaptist's Theology: Biblical, Historical, Constructive* (Downers Grove, Ill.: InterVarsity Press, 2004), pp. 246-54.

George Florovsky, *Creation and Redemption*, vol. 3, Collected Works (Belmont, Mass.: Nordland, 1976), pp. 189-200.

Stanley J. Grenz, *Theology for the Community of God* (Nashville: Broadman and Holman, 1994), pp. 603-31.

Shirley C. Guthrie, *Christian Doctrine*, revised edition (Louisville: Westminster/John Knox Press, 1994), pp. 363-72.

Robert W. Jenson, *Systematic Theology*, vol. 2, *The Works of God* (New York: Oxford University Press, 1999), pp. 178-200.

Michael Jinkins, *Invitation to Theology: A Guide to Study, Conversation & Practice*. Foreword by Alan Torrance (Downers Grove, Ill.: InterVarsity Press, 2002), pp. 226-32.

John H. Leith, *Basic Christian Doctrine* (Louisville: Westminster/John Knox Press, 1993), pp. 240-61.

James Wm. McClendon, Jr., *Systematic Theology*, vol. 2, *Doctrine* (Nashville: Abingdon Press, 1994), pp. 366-72, 477-82.

Daniel L. Migliore, *Faith Seeking Understanding: An Introduction to Christian Theology* (Grand Rapids: Eerdmans, 1991), pp. 189-205.

Jürgen Moltmann, *The Church in the Power of the Spirit: A Contribution to Messianic Ecclesiology*, trans. Margaret Kohl (New York: Harper & Row, 1977), pp. 337-61.

Dale Moody, *The Word of Truth: A Summary of Christian Doctrine Based on Biblical Revelation* (Grand Rapids: Eerdmans, 1961), pp. 427-33, 440-48.

Christopher Morse, *Not Every Spirit: A Dogmatics of Christian Disbelief* (Valley Forge: Trinity Press International, 1994), pp. 301-17.

Robert Cummings Neville, *A Theology Primer* (New York: State University of New York Press, 1991), pp. 153-66.

Thomas C. Oden, *Systematic Theology,* vol. 3, *Life in the Spirit* (San Francisco: HarperSanFrancisco, 1991), pp. 297-365.

Wolfhart Pannenberg, *Systematic Theology,* vol. 3, trans. Geoffrey W. Bromiley (Grand Rapids: Eerdmans, 1998), pp. 405-34.

Ted Peters, *God — The World's Future: Systematic Theology for a Postmodern Era* (Minneapolis: Fortress Press, 1992), pp. 292-305.

Letty M. Russell, *Human Liberation in a Feminist Perspective: A Theology* (Philadelphia: Westminster Press, 1974), pp. 155-63.

Ninian Smart and Steven Constantine, *Christian Systematic Theology in a World Context* (Minneapolis: Fortress Press, 1991), pp. 334-44.

Dorothee Soelle, *Thinking About God: An Introduction to Theology* (Philadelphia: Trinity Press International, 1990), pp. 141-53.

Marjorie Hewitt Suchocki, *God-Christ-Church: A Practical Guide to Process Theology* (New York: Crossroad, 1982), pp. 134-44.

Gordon J. Spykman, *Reformational Theology: A New Paradigm for Doing Dogmatics* (Grand Rapids: Eerdmans, 1992), pp. 440-60.

Otto Weber, *Foundation of Dogmatics,* vol. 2, trans. Darrell L. Guder (Grand Rapids: Eerdmans, 1983), pp. 552-66.

Geoffrey Wainwright, *Doxology: The Praise of God in Worship, Doctrine, and Life* (New York: Oxford University Press, 1980), pp. 118-38.

Among the systematics works in this period vis-à-vis the marks/attributes/signs, G. C. Berkouwer's volume on the church in his Studies in Dogmatics series is unique. The doctrine is explored by dividing the entire book into the four attributes:

G. C. Berkouwer, *The Church,* trans. James E. Davison (Grand Rapids: Eerdmans, 1976).

PART II

SEARCHING THE SIGNS

CHAPTER 4

Kerygma: *Proclamation and Apostolicity*

As noted in the discussion of *kerygma* in Chapter 3, one of the first concerns of the early generations of the Christian community was to discern where "church" was to be found. Thus emerged a "rule of faith" that distinguished the real thing from counterfeits.[1] The *regula fidei* soon appeared in various forms, with the Roman rule emblematic, a "canon of truth" that found its way into the writings of the early Fathers, notably Irenaeus and Tertullian, and was carried forward by later Fathers (viz., Origen). It arose as a way of condensing the core of the Scripture being read in the churches for the purposes of baptismal confession, preaching and catechesis, and also as an aid in polemics with those considered deviant in their teaching from the church catholic. So Irenaeus:

> This, then is the order of the rule of faith . . . God the Father, not made, not material, invisible; one God, the creator of all things; this is the first point of our faith. The second point is this: the Word of God, Son of God, Christ Jesus our Lord, Who was manifested by the prophets according to the form of prophesying and according to the methods of the Father's dispensation; through Whom (i.e. the Word)

---

1. The use of "rule" is interesting in the light of current statements noted earlier of some who declare that their church has no "rules."

all things were made. Who also at the end of the age, to complete and gather up all things, who was made man among men, visible and tangible, in order to abolish death and bring forth life and produce perfect reconciliation between God and man. And the third point is: the Holy Spirit, through whom the prophets prophesied, and the fathers learned the things of God, and the righteous were led into the way of righteousness; Who at the end of the age was poured out in a new way upon mankind in all the earth, renewing man to God.[2]

What we can learn from this early formulation is that (a) the church needed to identify its fundamental faith, with special reference to forces within its own ranks that had recourse to other criteria, ones drawn from the surrounding culture, especially Gnosticism; (b) the framework for such an identification was triadic — Father, Son, and Holy Spirit; (c) the triunity of God so affirmed was associated with the entry of believers into the church by baptism, and thus the trinitarian baptismal formula; (d) the Three-in-One referenced is treated narratively,[3] creation ascribed to the Father, reconciliation to the Son, and the application of the reconciliation wrought by the Son to persons and their "renewal" to the Holy Spirit. This history of God with us can be described, therefore, as a drama in three Acts;[4] (e) presupposed throughout, however, is the unity of the Persons in the doing of God as well as the being of God. Later, the triadic unity and triune narrativity came to be described as the immanent Trinity — the inner life of the triune God in such coinherence that the Three *are* One, and the economic Trinity — with the mission in each Act associated with the Persons, albeit entailing the participation of all, as "the works of the Trinity are one"; (f) this rule of faith, initially, and in its developed form, was viewed as "apostolic" in that it was a terse summary of the apostles' teaching, not that it was written by the apostles though some maintained such. Where this rule is followed, apostolicity is secured.

As can be seen, the early rule of faith grew over time into our present

---

2. Quoted in J. N. D. Kelly, *Early Christian Doctrines* (New York: Harper & Bros., 1958), p. 89.

3. "Narrative" being understood as a plot with characters moving over time and space through conflict toward resolution. See Gabriel Fackre, "Narrative Theology: An Overview," *Interpretation* 37, no. 4 (October 1983): 341.

4. So Bernhard W. Anderson, *The Unfolding Drama of the Bible,* 3rd edition (Minneapolis: Fortress Press, 1988).

"Apostles' Creed."[5] And to this, for purposes of further clarification of the gospel preached and taught in the church universal, an understanding of the work of the Holy Spirit was developed in more detail. In the light of the christological controversies of a yet later time, the "Nicene-Constantinopolitan Creed" sought to render patent what was latent in the Apostles' Creed, especially so the full deity of Jesus Christ:

> The only Son of God,
> Eternally begotten of the Father,
> God from God, Light from Light,
> True God from true God,
> Begotten not made,
> Of one Being with the Father. . . .

And yet again at the Council of Chalcedon in 451, further development of the import of both the deity and humanity of Jesus Christ was put in place in its Definition that since has achieved ecumenical consensus:

> Jesus Christ is the one and the same Son, the same perfect in God-head and the same perfect in manhood, truly God, and truly man, the same of rational soul and body, consubstantial with the Father in Godhead, and the same consubstantial with us in manhood, like us in all things, except sin; begotten of the Father before the ages as regards His Godhead, and in the last days, the same, because of us and because of our salvation begotten from the Virgin Mary, the *Theotokos*, as regards His manhood; one and the same Christ, Son, Lord, only-begotten, made known in two natures without confusion, without change, without division, without separation. . . .[6]

We shall return to the importance of this focus on the christological center of the creeds as we further investigate *kerygma*, the Word proclaimed, as a distinctive sign of the Spirit, attribute, and mark of the church. For now, a more extended look at the kerygmatic structure and meaning of the creeds.

---

5. For current commentary on the Apostles' Creed, see Roger E. Van Harn, ed., *Exploring and Proclaiming the Apostles' Creed* (Grand Rapids: Eerdmans, 2004) and Luke Timothy Johnson, *The Creed: What Christians Believe and Why It Matters* (New York: Doubleday, 2004).

6. Quoted in Kelly, *Early Christian Doctrines*, pp. 339-40.

To view the acts in the creedal drama through the lens of the Scripture from which they have arisen, scenes begin to appear. Creation is followed by the fall, the resistance of the world to the divine invitation. Yet the world does not cease to be but is sustained by a "common grace" of preservation set forth by a covenant with Noah. Then a special grace brings to be a "chosen people." Among them appears one of their own, Jesus the Jew, who is the Word enfleshed, living, teaching, healing, dying, and rising again in scenes in Galilee, Calvary, and on Easter morning. The church is birthed by the Holy Spirit descending from the ascended Christ on the day of Pentecost; its mission to the world is undertaken, with the proclamation and celebration of justifying and sanctifying graces. So the time between the Times, and then the End comes with its scenes of resurrection, return, judgment, and everlasting life. Transposing the dramatic change of scenes to a literary genre, we have a Story being told. A pastoral systematics as it is conceived in this series is the attempt at exposition of the Story/the Drama/the Creed for those who are called to share it ever and again from pulpit and lectern, in lesson and in life. Volume 1 in this series is an extended exploration of this Story. Rather than rehearsing its highlights here, they are presupposed in our discussion of *kerygma*.

The church exists where the *kerygma* happens, where the Word is proclaimed, and thus where apostolicity is to be found. The church is where the Storyline is faithfully followed, where no chapter is left out; or in the genre of the theater, no act or scene is omitted.

One way the church has sought to secure over time its apostolicity is to use the creeds in worship and instruction. For all the complaints about their time-boundedness, and given the need to reformulate the expression of their contents, or to update them in terms of new issues and idiom, and even with their omissions, they are historic markers of the church universal, and found in the confessional lore of most churches.[7] Their importance has to do with their witness to the core of Christian faith, a witness recognized by the church universal.

The creeds of the church are creatures of the Holy Spirit's work in the church, nodal points in the "tradition" that constitute a key resource to

---

7. Even the church most eager to keep in step with the times and not be bound by the past keeps in its Constitution the requirement to honor "the ancient creeds" and calls its constituency to attend to "this faith . . ." found there. Preamble to the Constitution of the United Church of Christ.

understanding and interpreting the biblical source.[8] As such, they not only derive from Scripture, but are accountable to it. As situated in the "world" and shaped by it, Scripture requires interpretation, the hermeneutical task taken up in Volume 2.[9] Indeed, in describing apostolic faith in the images of drama and story, we are seeking to be faithful to both contexting the meaning of *kerygma* in our own setting, and to grounding it in its biblical source. Hence, tradition in its varied forms, classic and contemporary, is a crucial, albeit corrigible element in discerning the kerygmatic mark of the church.

Alan Sell in an important work, *Confessing and Commending the Faith*, seeks to identify the *kerygma* common to the Christian community. In his quest for the defining characteristics of "confessing the faith" over time he inevitably turns to the role of creeds, yet with the appropriate cautions:

> What then of creeds and confessions? Do they then encapsulate the Church's confession? Yes and no. Certainly there is much to be said for the several churches' setting forth the faith commonly held in their midst . . . and those who would churlishly dispense with such statements on the ground of their antiquity should be warned by P. T. Forsyth that the iconoclasts do not always appear to understand that "it takes a great deal of theology to revolutionize theology." Yet . . . such documents are inevitably and properly the products of their time. . . . They have their proper but subordinate place. But to what are they subordinate? The answer can only be, to the Gospel as witnessed in Scripture. . . .[10]

Sell's search for the faith that is to be confessed takes him in the same direction as the Nicene fathers took the early formulation of apostolicity: the focus on the christological heart of the Story. What drives him there is his apologetic agenda. If the faith is to be commended, what is the faith that is to be confessed? Also, as a figure long active in the ecumenical movement, Sell is posing the question of what unifies the varied

---

8. *The Christian Story*, vol. 1, *A Narrative Interpretation of Basic Christian Doctrine*, 3rd edition (Grand Rapids: Eerdmans, 1996), *passim*.

9. *The Christian Story*, vol. 2, *Authority: Scripture in the Church for the World* (Grand Rapids: Eerdmans, 1987), *passim*.

10. Alan P. F. Sell, *Confessing and Commending the Faith: Historic Witness and Apologetic Method* (Cardiff: University of Wales Press, 2002), pp. 27, 29.

Christian traditions. His efforts to pin down what is essential in the kerygmatic center of Christian identity are illuminating, an attempt to answer the question posed at the end of his discussion of creeds as being accountable to the gospel, "And yet again the question arises: what is the gospel?"[11]

> The basic confession is that Jesus Christ is the crucified and risen Saviour. . . . Christianity's central piece of good news is that in Christ's death and resurrection God has done for us that which we could never have done for ourselves. . . . At the heart of the Christian confession is the announcement that Christ, and supremely in the cross-resurrection event, God has acted once and for all for the re-demption of the world.[12]

Sell's is one important effort to return to the christological center as the locus of what confessing in our time, or any time, entails.

The most influential twentieth-century move to a christocentric reading of the meaning of *kerygma* is found in the Barmen Declaration of 1934. The very "being" of the church in Germany was then at stake. Confessing required going to the "Center." In doing so, Barmen, significantly, begins with the four classical attributes of the church:

> We are united by our common Confession of the One Lord of the One, Holy, Catholic and Apostolic Church.

It interprets these defining characteristics in terms of "the common confession of the One Lord" in its Article 1:

> Jesus Christ, as He is testified to us in the Holy Scriptures, is the one Word of God, which we have to hear and which we have to trust and obey in life and in death.[13]

And it makes clear that this affirmation requires rejections as well as affirmations:

---

11. Sell, *Confessing and Commending the Faith*, p. 29.

12. Sell, *Confessing and Commending the Faith*, pp. 86, 35, 150.

13. Quoted from the Barmen Declaration in Arthur C. Cochane, *The Church's Confession Under Hitler* (Philadelphia: Westminster Press, 1962), pp. 237-42.

We reject the false doctrine that the Church can and must acknowledge as sources of its proclamation, except and beside this one Word
of God, other events and powers, forms and truths, as God's revelation.[14]

Thus the church under fire goes to the heart of the matter: Jesus Christ, the
one Word, as testified to in Scripture. While the principal author of the
Declaration, Karl Barth, was suspicious of the kind of apologetics called
for by Sell, at the end of the day, both turn to the christological center of
apostolic proclamation. Is it any accident that both had strong commitments to the ecumenical movement?

Putting this duality of *kerygma* into the language we are using, it can be
said that the proclamation of the gospel comes in both *long form* and *short
form*. The gospel in long form is the story of God from creation to consummation. The gospel in short form is its central chapter, Jesus Christ, the
Word enfleshed, living, dying, rising, and ruling. When the moment of decision comes as to where to draw the line in the sand — polemically, ecumenically, apologetically — it is at the centerpoint of the Story. But to understand what the meaning of the Center is, the full Tale must be told. And
to tell it, the classical creeds of the church that grew out of a universal
church constitute a fundamental resource. Subsidiary resources from the
tradition are subsequent confessions that lift up one or another aspect, so
elicited from the challenges of varied times and places, and formulated cor-
porately by communities of faith, rather than being individualistic profes-
sions. The ecumenical movement is the place where these enrichments and
enlargements are in dialogue, thus demonstrating the interrelationship of
koinonia and *kerygma*. Indeed, the fullness of the gospel only comes to us
through the wholeness of the church. Hence, the ecumenical imperative.

We cannot wait for the eschaton to establish, ecumenically, our fundamental kerygmatic identity and must settle for what is possible short of
that time when the church that God intends will be all in all even as God
will be all in all. This time between the Times requires the gospel in short
form as crucial to ecclesial identity, and the gospel in long form as the content for the full and fair reading of the center of the Story.

A dimension of the *kerygma* implicit in all the foregoing has yet to be
made explicit — in Barmen's language, "Jesus Christ, as testified to in Holy

---

14. *The Church's Confession Under Hitler*, pp. 237-42.

Scripture. . . ." The Story writ large or small, long form or short form, from beginning to End or at its Center, can only be found in the Book, the "Storybook." The Good News of Jesus Christ rises out of the full news of Scripture's narrative from Genesis to Revelation. Integral to the proclamation of the gospel is the biblical source of any tradition that has come to be as a resource to the preaching and teaching of the gospel.[15]

Karl Barth has expressed this threefold aspect of the *kerygma* as the three forms of the Word: the Word enfleshed, the Word preached, and the Word written. We have made reference to his witness to the first in drafting the Barmen Declaration, with its orientation point as "the one Word, Jesus Christ." That Word as proclaimed is the church's effort to witness to the one Word in its creeds, confessions, and restatements on which the day-to-day preaching and teaching of pastors draw. All of this body of teaching is accountable, finally, to Scripture, the Word written. Thus the first sign of the Spirit, its apostolicity, is where that threefold Word is faithfully proclaimed.[16]

As our examples of commitment to the *kerygma* illustrate — from the early creeds and church Fathers to Sell and Barth — confessing the faith with Christ as the Center puts one regularly on a collision course with the surrounding culture. Especially so when the ideologies of the day make their way into the preaching and teaching of the church. The contest with Gnosticism and the religion of the Roman state, as repudiated in the creedal and patristic declarations, and the juxtaposition of "Jesus is Lord" to "Caesar is Lord" in the primitive congregations, were early indications of how Christian confession had to resist cultural captivity, and the cost entailed in assertion of kerygmatic identity. It is no accident that both Barth in the Barmen Declaration vis-à-vis "German Christianity" and

15. Developed in vol. 2 of the *Christian Story* series, *Authority: Scripture in the Church for the World* (Grand Rapids: Eerdmans, 1987), pp. 341-50 and *passim*.

16. The Study Catechism adopted by the Presbyterian Church USA in 1998, and no little influenced by Barth, is a worthy current attempt to introduce both members and new members into the kerygmatic core. For the implications of what is entailed in a church that so confesses that faith — a "confessing church" — see the commentary of George Hunsinger, the principal drafter of the catechism, in his book *Disruptive Grace: Studies in the Theology of Karl Barth* (Grand Rapids: Eerdmans, 2000), especially the chapter "Barth, Barmen, and the Confessing Church Today," pp. 60-88. For another current attempt to reclaim *kerygma* in the mainline church, see the writings of Fleming Rutledge, especially her website, "Generous Orthodoxy."

Sell as theological secretary of the World Alliance of Reformed Churches vis-à-vis its expulsion of a South African church because of its racist ideology reflected the over-against-ness of faith and culture when premises from the latter took charge of the former. Faithfulness to the one Word is ever wary of the seductions of current ideology and must be ready for a costly discipleship.[17]

17. A current example of such is the letter of the Confessing Christ movement in the UCC to pastors and teachers on the anniversary of the Barmen Declaration:

"For everything there is a season, and a time for every matter under heaven: a time to weep, and a time to laugh; . . . a time to keep silence, and a time to speak." (Eccles. 3:1, 4, 7b)

In the face of events that are scalding the earth and fracturing the nations, we are thinking of each of you and asking ourselves, as you also are doing. . . . "How can those who confess Christ hold their tongues?" We remember you in our prayers as you preach, teach, and "equip the saints" for their ministry in times like these.

And we remember our Barmen forebears on this 70th anniversary of their "Declaration." Can they help us bear witness in our time, as they did in theirs:

— to "Jesus Christ, as he is attested for us in Holy Scripture . . . the one Word of God which we have to hear, and which we have to trust and obey in life and in death." (Article 1)?

— to say again loud and clear: "No other foundation can anyone lay than that which is laid, which is Jesus Christ." (1 Cor. 3:11)?

— and to find a way to "reject the false doctrine, as though the Church were permitted to abandon the form of its message and order to its own pleasure or to changes in prevailing ideological and political convictions." (Article 3)?

Confronting the "German Christians" and their fusion of blood and soil with the "one Word of God," Barmen spoke a bold "No!" Today, we have to do with "American Christians" who cannot separate nation from gospel, counting upon God to bless their crusades and praying to "Jesus, the warrior" rather than to "the Lamb of God who takes away the sin of the world." To this, we likewise speak a firm "No!" So also to any other ethnic or theocratic claim to hold hostage the sovereign God and view ourselves as a "righteous empire."

While the divine majesty is wrongly blended with national allegiances and ethnic loyalties, we know also that Jesus Christ is Lord of our lands as well as our souls. We ought not to be silent before the present tyrannies and injustices that abound on our own soil and in other nations. We encourage you to seek places in every congregation where the wounding of Christ and the folly of nations can be faced and the issues aired. We pray that you may find ways within the life of the congregations you serve to examine, as students of Scripture and as theologians, the inflamed situations described imperfectly every day in the media, risking judgments

Apostolicity and Its Interpretations

As noted, the early centuries of the church were marked by the effort to clarify its identity vis-à-vis its culture and competing worldviews. Crucial to that was continuity with the apostles themselves. Three indicators of that apostolicity were: the apostolic teaching, the apostolic writings, and the apostolic ministry.[18] Our attention here has been on apostolic teaching/proclamation. We have just noted its inseparability from the apostolic writings, the Word written as the habitat for the Word preached about the Word enfleshed. Therefore, implicit in all the foregoing is the assertion that the kerygmatic sign of the Holy Spirit constitutes the apostolicity of the church; the sign and the mark are one and the same. Where the Word is proclaimed, the Story told, there is found continuity with the apostles.

The early church knew, however, that the apostolic proclamation in writing and teaching required an apostolic stewardship comparable to the

---

and acting in humility rooted in the one Word of God each of us is called to proclaim.

While making our witness however, we acknowledge our own temptation to forget that "there is no one who is righteous, not even one!" (Rom. 3:10) Again, the wisdom of another forebear, Reinhold Niebuhr, is ours to learn. In the heat of the struggles of his day against the powers and principalities, he confessed to the sin that persists in the champions of justice as well as in its foes. He also prayed for forgiveness of his own self-righteous fury.

Along with the courage to speak and the contrition that must accompany it, comes the consoling Word spoken by another of our great teachers in an earlier time of tribulation. Writing to Christians in England as the bombs fell and the struggle against Hitler went forward, Karl Barth said that "the world in which we live is the place where Jesus Christ rose from the dead . . . although at present the glory of the Kingdom of God is held out to us only as a hope, yet the kingly rule of Christ extends over the whole of the universe . . . and confronts and overrules . . . the principalities and powers and evil spirits of this world." Amen!

There is a time for those who confess Christ to speak and there is a time to be silent. It is when we listen for the Word of God and look for light from this Source that we are able to discern the signs of the times. And so we pray for each of you and for the Church in whose midst we all kneel as servants: "Speak to us, O Lord, the Word we need and let that Word abide in us until it has wrought in us your holy will."

18. Traced out in Adolf Harnack, *Outlines of the History of Dogma,* Introduction by Philip Reiff, trans. Edwin Knox Mitchell (Boston: Beacon Press, 1957), pp. 84-100.

presence and persons of the original apostles. Hence the third form of identity-preservation, an apostolic *ministry*.

What is apostolic ministry? In the Roman Catholic Church it has come center stage, and is related to the foregoing dimension of apostolicity in this way:

> The Church has a threefold apostolicity: a) of doctrine in that she teaches the same as the Apostles taught; b) of mission or authority, in that she has inherited her mission and authority from the Apostles through a legitimate uninterrupted succession of pastors; c) of society in that she is the same society as that of which the Apostles were the foundation.[19]

Thus this church points in (a) to the apostolic teaching we have been exploring as the kerygmatic sign of the Holy Spirit, and adds a second and third qualification that relates to the Word proclaimed in the church discussed above. In actual practice, for Roman Catholic historical interpretation and ecumenical relationships, both the third and the first depend on the middle principle: apostolic succession in ministry. The faith and the society are secured by clergy in tactual continuity with the first pastors.

Those who do not subscribe to the way apostolic ministry is construed in the Roman Catholic tradition — episcopal order in continuity with first pastors led by a papacy — must acknowledge the importance of a point beneath the specific formulary: the need for stewardship of the mysteries within the church. Such began as an organ in the Body of Christ (1 Cor. 12), a cadre of

> some pastors and teachers, to equip the saints for the work of ministry, for building up the body of Christ . . . (Eph. 4:11-12)

The organ developed over time into an ordained office in the institution of the church. By the power of the Spirit, the community assigns to some the care and feeding of the Body with the food of *kerygma*.

The pastoral office is the stewardship of the "mysteries" (1 Cor. 4:1 KJV), custodianship of the *identity* of the church.[20] The pastor is called as

---

19. "Apostolicity," in Donald Attwater, ed., *A Catholic Dictionary*, 3rd edition (New York: Macmillan, 1961), p. 30.

20. *The Christian Story*, vol. 1, pp. 171-76.

principal caretaker of the message of the gospel and its meaning for a given time and place.[21] Is this organ the mouth in the Body that speaks the Word that tells the world who that Body is? (Luther's description of a church as a "mouthhouse" follows the figure.) Without such an organ the Body is speechless regarding the gospel, the knowledge of its identity unknown. Changing the metaphor to that of the epistle to the Ephesians, the saints remain unequipped for their own ministry without "pastors and teachers." The pastoral office is fundamental to the identity of the Body of Christ, of its *esse*. Of course, the divine freedom is such that "God is able from these stones to raise up children to Abraham" (Luke 3:8), an apostolic "church" happening where the Holy Spirit chooses to bring it to be.[22] While not exhaustive of the Holy Spirit's possibilities, since New Testament times pastoral stewardship of the mysteries is normative for the life of the church, an office necessary to keep the Body *alive*.

At the same time, there is another office that keeps the Body *alert*. Such is the ministry of the saints described in the Ephesians letter, the ministry of the "laity" called to enable the body to walk and work in the *world*. If the pastoral office is a ministry of *identity*, the laity office is a ministry of *vitality*.[23] A vital, healthy Body will move out of the mouthhouse exercising its calling beyond its doors. More about this in a section to come. For now, we attend to the custodianship of the church's identity through the calling of the pastor.

The church over time has interpreted the ministry of the pastoral office as threefold: prophetic, priestly, and royal. These dimensions of ministry,

21. See "The Church and the Ordained Ministry" in *Baptism, Eucharist and Ministry* (Geneva: World Council of Churches, 1982), pp. 21-24.

22. In some traditions, this leads to asserting that the pastoral office is of the *bene esse* not the *esse* of the church. "A Church being a company of people combined together by covenant for the worship of God, it appeareth thereby that there may be the essence & being of a church without any officers seeing there is both the form and matter of a church, which is implied when it is said, the Apostles ordained elders in every church. . . . Nevertheless, though officers be not absolutely necessary, to the simple being of churches, when they be called: yet ordinarily to their calling they are, and to their well-being and therefore the Lord Jesus out of his tender compassion hath appointed and ordained officers which he would not have done, if they had not been useful and needfull for the church." "The Cambridge Platform," in Williston Walker, *Creeds and Platforms of Congregationalism* (Boston: Pilgrim Press, 1960), p. 210. Again, the Society of Friends and the Salvation Army are the exceptions that prove the rule.

23. *The Christian Story*, vol. 1, pp. 170-76.

however described (viz., in the Roman tradition — magisterial, sacerdotal, and jurisdictional), carry us beyond the present focus on *kerygma* and we shall follow it to the other reaches, but it does include the prophetic office of declaring the Word, proclaiming the gospel and teaching its content. The pastor is called to throw the faith joyfully in the air for the congregation to see it and believe it.

In order for the full Story to be told, preaching and teaching are best done by following the church year with its rounded account of the Grand Narrative with the Jesus chapter at its center, lections developed ecumenically, seeking thus to be faithful to that fullness. Other aspects of life in the parish are ways of teaching the faith, ones that will take us into the other attributes of the church — teaching opportunities, worship and sacraments, life and witness. At this point, however, we fix upon the critical role of the pastor in the task of proclaiming the gospel in the Word preached, a continuation in apostolic ministry of custodianship of the apostolic teaching.

But questions remain. What of the specific form of apostolic ministry represented by the greater part of the Christian community today, with Roman Catholic, Orthodox, and Anglo-Catholic traditions deeming such apostolicity to be the *esse* of the Body's life? "Apostolic succession" only warranting a faithful pastoral office? Here the church catholic must heed the Reformation concern. For all its variations, there was a common mind. The episcopal office as operative in the Roman Catholic Church of that day did not faithfully guard the apostolic faith and secure the apostolic society by its apostolic ministry. Hence that office could not be deemed of the essence of the church. Rather, the church exists in assembly anywhere the Word is faithfully preached and the sacraments rightly administered, whether in or out of churches that lay claim to tactual continuity with the first apostles.[24] History has borne out this Reformation conviction, given the dramatic manifestation of faithful witness beyond the borders of churches with episcopal continuity, a fact increasingly recognized by the Roman Catholic Church itself, even when it is willing only to name those

---

24. So Article 7 of the Augsburg Confession. See Robert Kolb and Timothy J. Wengert, eds., *The Book of Concord: The Confessions of the Evangelical Lutheran Church*, trans. Charles Arand, Eric Gritsch, Robert Kolb, William Russell, James Schaaf, Jane Strohl, and Timothy J. Wengert (Minneapolis: Fortress Press, 2000), p. 42: "It is the assembly of all believers among whom the gospel is purely preached and the holy sacraments are administered according to the gospel."

locales as "ecclesial communities" and not "churches."[25] And now to be further taken into account is the notable spread, vitality, and teaching faithfulness in churches with no relationship to the Reformation any more than to Roman Catholic and Eastern Orthodox traditions.[26] There is current evidence of faithful and vital congregations with pastors that more than a few times spring up without any standard credentialing or preparation. Indeed, no little of the ferment in the non-western church world appears to be of this sort.[27] Further, the commitment to classical Christian teaching in the mainline churches where continuity of one sort or another is present, is less and less evident, as the story of recent decades indicates. The institutions that prepare persons for ordained ministry and the denominational gatekeepers reflect the same weakening of witness to the *kerygma*.[28] One of the struggles in mainline churches at the beginning of the twenty-first century is whether, and if so how, to make a place in the ordination process for those with no formal training in the received educational route to ordination, but who give other evidence of qualities traditionally associated with the pastoral office.[29]

Given the existence of apostolic teaching outside those churches in apostolic succession (and thus actually in apostolic succession of "doctrine"), it is also true that extra-succession traditions have become, from time to time, captive to the contexts in which they reside, having no accountability to the learnings of the more structured church universal. Thus we have

25. See The Congregation for the Doctrine of the Faith, *Dominus Iesus*, August 6, 2000.

26. Philip Jenkins, *The Next Christendom: The Coming of Global Christianity* (New York: Oxford University Press, 2002).

27. Jenkins, *The Next Christendom*.

28. The American Academy of Religion, which is a showcase of the doctrine taught in seminaries and university divinity schools as well as in religious studies programs in colleges, gives little encouragement to the view that the stewards of identity trained by these teachers will indeed carry out this commission. See, for example, the self-examination done by a committee of the AAR in 2005.

29. The issue came home to the United Church of Christ in its 2005 General Synod, comparable to that of other mainline denominations considering a second non-seminary track of clergy preparation. One of the ironies in the UCC case is that the new ethnic clergy for which room is sought by alternate experiential routes to ordination may well bring with them more commitment to classical Christian teaching from their evangelical habitat than may come from the usual standard advanced educational preparation, to which they have not had access. And irony upon irony, these clergy are not sought for that reason but because of the regnant notion of "diversity."

learned from history not only of the fallibility of claims to preserve the church's kerygmatic identity by an inherited system of ordered ministry, but also the dangers of the loss of kerygmatic integrity when there is ministerial disorder. The evidence of such a need is everywhere to be seen in congregations that materialize and de-materialize by virtue of "charismatic" preachers who have no credentials other than those created by themselves or their congregations and whose idiosyncratic "doctrine" bears little resemblance to classical Christian teaching.[30] What then is the alternative?

An alternative must take into account two considerations. The first is suggested by the Roman Catholic claim of apostolicity of ministry as related to a "society" in continuity with the Apostles. Such an alternative would reject the delimitation of that continuity to the Roman Catholic Church, but acknowledge the value in a pastoral stewardship of the gospel in "organic" relationship to the Apostles. With the New Testament images of mustard seed and vine and branches, as well as body, the church can be understood as a continuous growth nurtured by the Holy Spirit and assured of its continuing life by Christ's promise of his unfailing presence. Thus it is the Spirit of the Son of the Father that sustains the Body since its beginning, and maintains always the organs integral to its life. One of those organs is the ministry of Word and Sacrament. It is not guaranteed by any organization, papal or otherwise, but by the living organism that the church is. Some form of ministry has always been part of the Body of Christ and contributed its charism to that ongoing life, continuing in different forms in the varied branches from the one vine, Jesus Christ. Therefore, this stream of continuity in the processes of preparation and validation is not to be disdained. Even as ministries of preaching and worship flourish outside of the historic churches and their ordaining procedures, the latter are important custodians of apostolic teaching, however lackluster their performance compared to the vitalities in congregations with less regularized clergy.[31]

30. Tony Campolo has an interesting exchange with his son who left his denomination for a megachurch, arguing that even in the lackluster mainline churches, there is formal stewardship of classical teaching and thus some historic touchstones for the pastoral office and a congregation's faith. See Tony Campolo, *Can Mainline Denominations Make a Comeback?* (Valley Forge, Pa.: Judson Press, 1995), pp. 3-12 and *passim.*

31. All denominations now face such debates about the equivalency of experience and education in clergy training requirements for ordination.

On the larger issue of the continuity of ministry through the organism, not the organi-

Second, in the light of the present kerygmatic incoherence noted earlier, an argument can be made for the more traditional threefold ordering of the pastoral office (bishop, presbyter, deacon), not as of the *esse*, but of the *bene esse* of the church. The merits of such a form of ministry, one that includes episcopacy in presumed continuity with the apostles, are now acknowledged by such ecumenical developments as the "Churches of Christ Uniting" in North America with reference to its earlier document, *The COCU Consensus*, the nine denominations covenanted to be together at some point in some form in the future.[32] The same thing is true in important bilateral agreements both national and international.[33] As to interpreting the premise underlying these agreements, it might be said that those churches willing to enter into relationships with others that lay claim to episcopal succession assume not only that there are benefits to stewarding the faith in times of theological disarray by having an episcopal office, but that ecumenically considered any fuller realization of the goal of ecumenism must include such a component. Apostolic ministry in its ecumenical reach, both latitudinally and longitudinally, cannot, finally, be "well" without a threefold ministry in apostolic succession. Nothing is taken away from churches that do not have such, for it is not of the *esse* of "church"; only the pastoral office as such is. *How* an episcopal ministry is to be executed, of course, is integral to any positive ecumenical response. As all of the current explorations indicate, a truly ecumenical episcopacy must be what it was originally in the ministry of Christ, a servant not the lord of its vineyard, in this case a resource to the work and witness of the pastor in the assembly of the faithful, with no imperial pretensions.

Another way of construing this question is to identify the three expressions of ordained ministry in the history of the church as *sacramental, organic,* and *experiential.* The first holds authentic ministry of this sort as entry into "the Sacrament of Holy Orders"[34] established by apostolic

---

zation, of the church, see the writings of the Mercersburg theologians. For example, "The Holy Ministry," in Emmanuel V. Gerhard, *Institutes of the Christian Religion,* vol. 2, with an Introduction by Philip Schaff (New York: Funk & Wagnalls Co., 1894), pp. 509-52.

32. See "The Threefold Pattern of Ordained Ministry," in *The COCU Consensus,* in *Churches in Covenant Communion and The COCU Consensus,* combined edition (Princeton: Consultation on Church Union, rev. ed. 1995), pp. 47-55.

33. As for example, the North American Episcopal-Lutheran "Called to Common Mission."

34. Article 6, "The Sacramental Economy," *Catechism of the Catholic Church,* pp. 383-89.

succession. The second dissociates it from the specificity of tactual succession through bishops while holding to apostolic continuity through the life of Christ in the Body which sets apart by ordination some to an "office" (not an "order" in apostolic succession) for the stewardship of Word and Sacrament.[35] The third has no brief for historic continuity through either order of office, but looks to the signs of capacity to steward *kerygma* and *leitourgia* wherever discerned and validates them accordingly, "apostolic success" as it has been described. Is there a way for the mainline Protestant churches that, by and large, represent the "organic" view of ordained ministry to make room for the insights of both the structures of the sacramental and the spontaneities of the experiential?

Yet a final question vis-à-vis the original formulation of apostolic succession in Roman Catholic idiom: What of the papacy? As in the Reformation rejection of that office as a failed venture in doctrinal oversight that prompted the departure of the Reformation churches and sequel traditions from its jurisdiction, the papacy cannot be construed as of the *esse* of the pastoral office. The church exists in kerygmatic faithfulness without either the order of episcopacy or its papal officer. However, if the church ecumenical is to be a reality, it must include one half of the membership as now represented by the Roman Catholic Church. As that church defines itself by its relationship to Rome, no church catholic could ever exist without incorporating in some way the charism the Roman part of the Christian community would choose to bring to a church ecumenical. Further, there is an argument to be made in this time and place, and future times and places, in which human challenges — political, sociological, technological, philosophical, political, and religious — are in the nature of the case globalized, requiring thereby a global voice for the universal church. Such would work, again, for the *well-being,* not the being, of the church's life and witness. Those in both the non-papal Reformation and Orthodox churches should put this question on the table of ecumenical negotiations and not preclude it a priori. Indeed, those two streams of Christianity by their establishment of the World Council of Churches tacitly acknowledge that a world presence and voice are needed for the well-being of the church at large. The WCC has not proven over time always to be what its pioneers sought. That does not, however, prevent its return to

---

35. The term "office" rather than "order" is pervasive in Protestant rites of ordination and manuals of interpretation.

the 1961 vision, itself open to the present argument, and in such a way that it could press the Roman Catholic Church to rethink how the papacy might be re-conceptualized in terms of a resource to the ministry and mission of the church and not the source of its self-definition. Already there are indications of such an openness in the document, *Ut Unum Sint*.[36] So re-conceptualized and renewed, the papacy also might be considered of the *bene esse* of the church and its ministry. Let the conversation go forward.[37]

The Ministry of the Laity

Another question that remains in exploring the apostolic ministry, again in its fullness, is "the ministry of the whole people of God," that whole including 99 percent who do not occupy the pastoral office: the ministry of the laity. We have already spoken of it as an office in its own right, the "ministry of vitality," partner to the pastoral "ministry of identity." How does this ministry relate to the concept of apostolic ministry?

Interestingly, the Roman Catholic Church has said at its Second Vatican Council that the laity exercise the threefold ministry of prophet, priest, and king,[38] and identify such as an "apostolate." Thus, in some sense, the laity participate in the defining mark of apostolicity. The Reformation anticipated this same inclusive view, as in the Heidelberg Catechism, which in the answer to Question 31 identifies Christ the Anointed One as carrying forward the three offices of the Old Testament prophets, priests, and kings, and then asks in Question 32, "Why are you called a Christian?" answering,

> Because through faith I share in Christ and thus his anointing that I may confess his name, offer myself as a living sacrifice of gratitude to him and fight against sin and the devil. . . .

36. See Carl E. Braaten and Robert W. Jenson, eds., *Church Unity and the Papal Office: An Ecumenical Dialogue on John Paul II's Encyclical* Ut Unum Sint (Grand Rapids: Eerdmans, 2001).

37. And it has. So the issue of *The Christian Century,* captioned "Protestants and the Pope" with an argument for Protestant openness made by D. Stephen Long, "Protestants and the Papacy: In Need of a Pope?" *The Christian Century* 122, no. 10 (May 17, 2005): 10-11.

38. "Decree on the Apostolate of the Laity," *The Documents of Vatican II,* ed. Walter Abbott, S.J. (New York: Association Press, 1966), p. 491.

Thus all of the church, by baptism and faith, continue the threefold office of Jesus Christ. As such, the ministry of the laity is also of the *esse* of the church.

How does the ministry of the laity contribute, or does it, to the Spirit's kerygmatic sign? Again we turn to the Roman Catholic arena, which has placed such importance on apostolicity in ministry. The prophetic office of the laity has to do with

> a true apostolate for opportunities to announce Christ by words addressed either to non-believers with a view to leading them to faith, or to believers with a view to instructing and strengthening them and motivating them toward a more fervent life.[39]

While the tip point of the prophetic office is seen to be in the mission of the laity outside the church, in this kerygmatic case in evangelism, there is also a kerygmatic role within the church for the lay apostolate, a role of instruction and strengthening. Historically, this has expressed itself in powerful lay movements that are focused on theological and spiritual renewal within the church. But behind this, one cannot but wonder if the authors of this document on the lay apostolate had in mind the longtime teaching within their church of the *sensus fidelium*. That is, the doctrine that is officially declared or interpreted by clerical organs of the church, the bishops in council or the pope, is not without relationship to the *sensus,* even the *consensus,* of the faithful as they practice and speak about their faith, and that ferment from below rising to the decision-making levels of their church's life. So, for example, the piety of the faithful was a key ecclesial factor and perhaps even the fountainhead of the mariological doctrines declared by the episcopacy as authoritative.[40]

The counterpart in the Reformation tradition of lay involvement in the *kerygma* is the expectation that the faithful will "confess his name" and do that as the leading edge of evangelization, inasmuch as the ministry of the laity is first and foremost in the world.[41] However, in the Reformation tra-

---

39. "Decree on the Apostolate of the Laity," p. 496.

40. For a notable discussion, see John Henry Newman, *On Consulting the Faithful in Matters of Doctrine,* with an Introduction by John Coulson (London, 1961), reissued with a Foreword by Derek Worlock, Archbishop of Liverpool (London, 1986).

41. So argued in the writer's "Christ's Ministry and Ours," in George Peck and John S. Hoffman, eds., *The Laity in Ministry: The Whole People of God for the Whole World* (Valley Forge, Pa.: Judson Press, 1984), pp. 109-25.

dition, where the Spirit is believed to be active among the people and where such is lived out by the leadership of laity in Christian education venues, in "spiritual councils" within the church, and movements of spiritual renewal, Bible study and theological concern for the integrity of faith, there is a kerygmatic role *within* the church as well. Indeed, the laity were critical to the Reformation fires that swept through the sixteenth century.

How are these apostolic ministries related in their exercise of the prophetic office — the relation of the ministries of the pastor and the laity? As noted above, the pastoral office is the charism in the Body of Christ called to continuously guard the faith of the church in its preaching and teaching. But the faith it guards cannot be without the consent, consensus, and counsel of the whole people of God, and thus the full range of its membership. The Holy Spirit is given to that whole Body and all of its parts to support, sustain, and to be in dialogue with the pastoral guardians and prime communicators of the gospel within the community of faith.[42] Time and again, the history of the church has illustrated the importance of the pastoral office in the exercise of its role when the church's teaching was threatened by Babylonian captivity. And in other times and places, the role of the laity was crucial in reminding the pastoral office of the faith that it is called to announce, and the need for its contextuality in the world, in which the laity live, has been demonstrated. Indeed, the very image of the church as the Body of Christ points to the circulation of the "blood" of Christian truth throughout the whole organism, the "mouth" of proclamation not severed from the Body as a whole.[43]

Orders

In the history of the church, certain sub-communities have emerged with a specificity of purpose and distinctive discipline: "Franciscan," "Dominican," "Cistercian," etc. in the Roman Catholic Church, monastic orders within Eastern Orthodoxy, sisterhoods and brotherhoods within the Ref-

42. On the "mutuality" of ministries — laity and pastoral — see "Christ's Ministry and Ours," pp. 113-15.

43. For an earlier determination to give full attention to the ministry of the laity, albeit in nineteenth-century terms, see the Mercersburg theology known otherwise for its "high" doctrine of ordained ministry as in Gerhard, *Institutes of the Christian Religion*, vol. 2, pp. 509-43.

ormation traditions,[44] "para-church" organizations within evangelicalism, and "intentional communities" made up of "new monastics" in the left-wing Reformation tradition.[45] A case could be made that the emergence of Protestant denominations itself reflects the impulse within the Body of Christ to ensure that one or another aspect of its life (organ?) receive due attention with associated custodianship of its graces.

In Chapter 3 Avery Dulles's "models" of the church were examined. They also can be construed as a way of stewarding gifts given to the people of God. Does the correlation of the models with the signs of the Spirit suggest that the church requires in some form special companies within its life raised up for such stewardship? That these are "orders," whether labeled as such or not, born of the Spirit and integral to the ongoing life of the Body?

The same question might be asked of periods of church history, short or long. Does the Holy Spirit bring to the fore in a given time and place one or another of its signs as that is meet for the day? So it would seem from the "signs of the times" surveyed in Chapter 2, the church of a particular time constituting itself as an "order" of the day. A case might even be made that the sequencing of the accent on the apostolic mark of *kerygma,* as the culmination of the four decades of varied emphases, suggests that earlier accents in the preceding decades — especially the "subjective" ones of holiness and unity — require a clear grounding in the objective ones of catholicity and apostolicity. So believed many of those who pressed for the doctrinal foundations of action in the theological renewal movements and doctrinal accents of the 1980s. "Orders" in space and time have their place in the church, with due recognition of their relativity and their reductionist temptations in a Body with many parts.

*   *   *

We have searched in this section for an understanding of this critical sign of the Spirit, attribute and mark of the church — the proclamation of the gospel, the telling of the Story, the communication of the Word. As in our account of the pentecostal origins of the Christian church, the proclama-

---

44. The "Order of Corpus Christi," begun within the United Church of Christ out of the tradition of the Mercersburg theology with a rigorous discipline of prayer, liturgy, and sacrament, now includes those from other Protestant traditions as well.

45. See Jason Byassee, "The New Monastics," *The Christian Century* 122, no. 21 (October 18, 2005): 38-47.

tion/telling/communication has the twin dimensions of inreach and out-reach. The former takes shape in the preaching and teaching that goes on in the church local and in the church at large. The latter is manifest in evangelization and in the kind of witness made by the drafters of the Barmen Declaration. Our accent has been on the fullness of the Good News, its Grand Narrative with its central chapter, the cruciality of the full Book from which it rises, and the fullness of the ministry that is the caretaker of the Good News, in the being and well-being of the ministries of identity and vitality.

The images of the church in the New Testament are ways in which the attribute of apostolicity is given expression. The confession of three acts in the creedal drama that constitute the gospel in "long form" flow from the triune Life Together. The church of apostolicity is, therefore, the *people* of the triune God in both economy and ontology. In their humanity this people — we people — falter and fail in our stewardship of these mysteries, but the faithful God does not give up on the church and the gospel goes forth even in our fitful Tale-telling.

The apostolic church is the *Body* of Christ, for the gospel in "short form" is at the center of our Story: Christ, the one Word, heard ever and again in our midst. As a body of humans we regularly garble the good Word. But the Head cannot be separated from the Body and the Word will break through even the distorted noises we make in our "mouthhouses."

The apostolic church is a *Temple* of the Spirit where the gift of proclamation is given — from Peter's first homily to our labors on and in last Sunday's sermon. The temple has its shaky columns, formed too often by the cheap cement of our ideologies. But the temple belongs to the Spirit; the sign will be given, and the structure will stand.

CHAPTER 5

Leitourgia: *Celebration and Catholicity*

I n Chapter 3, "catholicity" was associated with something more than the geography of one institution. The understanding of its universality, as Berkouwer expresses it in describing a similar ecumenical trend,

> led to deeper reflection on the meaning of catholicity according to its qualitative grade, starting from the origin and mystery of the Church, her "being" in the world, apart from her varying exten-sion. . . . The necessity of reflecting more deeply on the dimension of depth in catholicity was felt.[1]

Here we locate that "depth" in worship and its central eucharistic act.

Leitourgia, liturgy — the "work of the people" in worship. Thomas Torrance describes liturgy as it was understood by early Christians as

> the corporate activity of the Church in worshipping God with its mind as well as its body, through humble repentance, adoration and praise, and thankful enjoyment of God in his transcendence, holiness and beauty.[2]

1. G. C. Berkouwer, *The Church,* trans. James E. Davison (Grand Rapids: Eerdmans, 1976), p. 110.

2. Thomas Torrance, *Karl Barth: Biblical and Evangelical Theologian* (Edinburgh: T. & T. Clark, 1990), p. 50.

At the heart of this encompassing life of *leitourgia* is the "Divine Liturgy," as the central act of worship is named in Eastern Orthodoxy.[3] And in the Roman Catholic Church, "it's the mass that matters." In both, the Meal is for those who have had the Bath, the eucharist as for the baptized faithful.[4] In the Reformation churches, the sacraments are also at the center as the "means of grace" along with the preaching of the gospel. In the companion communities — Roman and Eastern — the Mass and Liturgy in their fullest also entails the gospel proclaimed in homily and lection as well as in bread and wine.

Why this duet, this linkage of Word with bread and wine? The gospel of God proclaimed is witness to Jesus Christ. The worship of God in liturgical life is communication, that is, communion with Jesus Christ. Outreach and inreach, the horizontal and the vertical, the companionship of the means of grace, indeed their cruciformity and thus their christological import. The commonality and diversity are expressed by their description as the Word audible and the Word visible. In these two signs of the Spirit, we have Jesus Christ among us, constitutive of the being of his Body.

These two sign/marks came into prominence in the Reformation as those restive with the ecclesial givens asked ever and again, "Where is the church?" Where is the Body of Christ alive? The Augsburg Confession represented the common conclusion:

> It is also taught that at all times there must be and remain one holy, Christian church. It is the assembly of all believers among whom the gospel is purely preached and the holy sacraments are administered according to the gospel. For this is enough for the true unity of the Christian church. . . .[5]

From another translation of "this is enough," the *satis est* — "it is sufficient" — became a phrase used in ecumenical negotiations to establish

---

3. See *The Divine Liturgy,* N. Michael Vaporis, ed., English edition (Brookline, Mass.: Holy Cross Orthodox Press, 1983).

4. As in the completion of the "Christian initiation." See Article 3, paragraph 1322, "The Sacrament of the Eucharist," *Catechism of the Catholic Church,* English translation (Liguori, Mo.: Liguori Publications, 1994), p. 334.

5. Article 7, "Concerning the Church," *The Augsburg Confession,* in Robert Kolb and Timothy J. Wengert, eds., *The Book of Concord: The Confessions of the Evangelical Lutheran Church,* trans. Charles Arand, Eric Gritsch, Robert Kolb, William Russell, James Schaaf, Jane Strohl, and Timothy J. Wengert (Minneapolis: Fortress Press, 2000), p. 42.

"full communion."[6] The sufficiency of their presence to establish the being of the church has to do with the presence of the Word, Jesus Christ. Where he is in proclamation and rite, in the audibilities and visibilities, there is the church. Yes, there are other movements of the Spirit within the Body. But Word and sacrament are signs of its very life, of *keeping* it alive. The Body requires a Head and the Head has a mouth that utters the Word and is fed by the Meal.

The constituting partnership of *kerygma* and *leitourgia* is further indicated by their association with the pastoral office. In all traditions, the pastor is called to preach the gospel and preside at the Table. Conjoined in the eucharist, here happens the principal stewardship of the meanings and the mysteries of the faith, the Word proclaimed and celebrated. In terms of the threefold ministry of Christ, the *leitourgia* of the Table is the continuation of the priestly office in its pastoral form. "Priesting" has the eucharist at its center, but of course takes place in a variety of liturgical ways. Thus we turn now to worship in both its central and circumferential senses, initially attending to its sacramental core, then moving to the larger range of worship life.

The Sacraments

The number of sacraments remains a point of difference within the church universal, as does their naming. Nonetheless, the Bath and the Meal enjoy an ecumenical focus and even a convergence of understanding, including general agreement on their description as "sacraments," although some traditions prefer the language of "ordinance."

Early in Reformation teaching, and still today in some places, the case of baptism and eucharist as sacraments is made on the basis of their "dominical institution": Jesus stipulated and modeled for his followers these two acts by his own baptism and by his service at the first Table. However, what then of other acts that are enjoined upon us dominically — for example, foot-washing or going out two by two to share the Good News — but not given similar defining prominence? Other grounds are needed to establish these two rites as special means of liturgical grace.

---

6. Article 7 was key to the 1997 North American Lutheran-Reformed Formula of Agreement.

Ecumenical warrants are at hand in the Lima document in which "Baptism" and "Eucharist" are singled out for in-depth attention, with the associated pastoral relationship, "Ministry," being the third area of inquiry. The official responses to the Lima document from churches around the world in six succeeding volumes further illustrate their singular role.

The liturgical primacy of these two sacraments is grounded in their theological meaning. They have to do with the *birth* and the *nurture* of the Body of Christ. Without the natal waters and the food and drink at the Table, there would be no Body. In similar metaphor, the bathing of the newborn and its feeding are necessary for its life and health. The nexus between Bath and Meal are integral to the being of the church. Their presence and bonding are the way the Spirit brings the Body to be and sustains it. As there is no Bath and Meal without the Word spoken as well as seen, the verbal and visible are inextricable.

Before we examine the particulars of baptism and eucharist, the relation of this sacramental center of *leitourgia* to its liturgical circumference must be clarified. If, as an exhortation in the Order for Holy Communion of one tradition expresses it, "The celebration of the Lord's Supper has ever been regarded by the Church as the innermost sanctuary of the whole Christian worship,"[7] then what lies in the regions outside that sanctuary but within the worship walls of the church?

Employing another figure to relate center to circumference, we speak of both the length and width of the liturgical work of the Holy Spirit in the church. The length has to do, now, with members of the Body and the points in their pilgrimage. Stated otherwise, the church mothers its children, not only in childhood, as with human maternity, but throughout life — from birth to death.[8] Seen in this perspective, there is a sequence of the rites of the church (all considered by Roman and Eastern traditions as sacraments, while for the Reformation churches two sacraments and five rites) that accords with the "common ventures of life." For birth — bap-

---

7. "The Order for Holy Communion," *The Hymnal: Evangelical and Reformed Church* (St. Louis: Eden Publishing House, 1941), p. 21.

8. The "mothering" imagery comes naturally in ecclesiology as with John Calvin. But also it is interesting that thinkers as diverse as evangelical Donald Bloesch and ecumenical Robert Jenson take up Mariology in conjunction with their treatments of the doctrine of the church. See Donald Bloesch, *The Church: Sacraments, Ministry, and Mission* (Downers Grove, Ill.: InterVarsity Press, 2002), pp. 42, 64-67, 258-59, and Jenson, *Systematic Theology*, vol. 2, *The Works of God* (New York: Oxford University Press, 1999), pp. 200-204.

tism; for growth — confirmation; for nurture — eucharist; for support — confession and counsel; for vocation — ordination to multiple ministries;[9] for conjugal life together and its issue — marriage; for death — burial and/ or last rites. While the ritualizing of the turning points on the human pilgrimage are described differently, they do occur in virtually every Christian tradition. All are part of the length of the pilgrimage each member of the Body must take, validated accordingly in varied forms of personally diachronic *leitourgia.*

Liturgy happens in width as well as length. Here we have to do with the range of verticality, communion with Jesus Christ writ large — prayer and worship in its many and varied expressions. Its width has to do not only with the spectrum of locales represented — from private prayer to public worship, but also with the rich diversity of orientations to God within that span of Christian piety and practice. As is the case with *kerygma,* so with *leitourgia,* there may be found in Scripture a locus where in brief compass all the elements are present. So it is argued in Russell Mitman's *Worship in the Shape of Scripture.*[10] Mitman deals specifically with "the service of Word and Sacrament," but the framework can be extended to include other forms of *leitourgia,* from personal prayer to corporate worship of many kinds. In this framework, the range is represented by the moves of the heart of the worshiper in the temple as recorded in Isaiah 6:1-8. They can be characterized as adoration, confession, pardon, thanksgiving, petition, and intercession, hearing and answering the call.[11]

We shall return to these longer and wider reaches of *leitourgia,* but first to its central mysteries, the Bath and the Meal.

---

9. And why not a commissioning service for laity who construe their vocation as ministry, parallel to the ordination of clergy? Such was argued in the Center for the Ministry of the Laity at Andover Newton Theological School, recognizing that baptism is itself also "ordination" to vocation.

10. See F. Russell Mitman, *Worship in the Shape of Scripture* (Cleveland: The Pilgrim Press, 2001), p. 53. See also Dorothy and Gabriel Fackre, *Christian Basics: A Primer for Pilgrims* (Grand Rapids: Eerdmans, 6th printing, 2000), pp. 102-11.

11. Mitman constitutes them differently given his sacramental context with the action of communion being the personal encounter with Christ in the Word addressed and received. To the extent that the life of prayer and worship is itself an encounter with Christ of a different order than Word and Sacrament, what occurs paradigmatically and centrally in the means of grace is echoed and given wider though thinner range in the derivative acts of verticality.

The Meanings of Baptism

In the years immediately following the first assembly of the 1948 World Council of Churches, cited earlier as a thread leading to this work, the Faith and Order Commission of the WCC reported a "spectacular revival of interest in the subject of Christian initiation in some circles. . . ."[12] Why? The reason given was that "baptism is not only important in itself, but closely related to the broader question of the unity of the Church."[13] A participant in the discussion then presciently declared that in the midst of the ferment, "present developments make it clear that the future will see such discussions on a scale and in an atmosphere never before achieved."[14] The new level of churchwide concern and the forecast of promising achievements did make for an "ecumenical moment."[15] The fruit of the deep and wide dialogue was the 1982 Faith and Order Commission document, *Baptism, Eucharist and Ministry*, with its own worldwide impact. What follows draws on the twentieth-century exploration of that formative study.

Baptism's plural meanings are related to the diverse characterization of it in Scripture (Rom. 6:3-5; Col. 2:12; John 3:5; Eph. 5:15; Gal. 3:27; Titus 3:5; 1 Peter 3:20-21; 1 Cor. 10:1-2; Gal. 3:27-28; 1 Cor. 12:13).[16] Various baptismal traditions grow out of the accents in the one image of the "washing," though in many churches its multiple meanings are referenced, the ecumenical conversation witnessing to the richness of the rite.

The multiplicity of significances is grounded in the universal formula itself. The one God is at the same time three Persons. Thus the unity in usage of a formula that points to the rich diversity within the divine being lays the groundwork for the quest for a like richness in meanings of baptism in the divine name.

---

12. World Council of Churches Faith and Order Commission, *One Lord, One Baptism* (Minneapolis: Augsburg Publishing House, 1960), p. 45.

13. WCC, *One Lord, One Baptism*, p. 45.

14. Stephen J. England, *The One Baptism* (St. Louis: Bethany Press, 1960), p. 7.

15. See Geoffrey Wainwright, *The Ecumenical Moment: Crisis and Opportunity for the Church* (Grand Rapids: Eerdmans, 1983). The writer took part in a small ecumenical venture in the exploration of the meaning of baptism as faculty resource in an inter-seminary student inquiry in 1961 in the eastern Pennsylvania region. Out of it grew *The Baptismal Encounter*, Lancaster Theological Seminary Occasional Paper No. 1 (Lancaster, Pa.: Lancaster Theological Seminary, 1961).

16. Texts so cited by *BEM*, p. 2.

Ironically, the unity and universality of the formula are currently in question for some who demand the exclusion of biblical terms that appear to sanction patriarchy. The removal of the biblical and historical language has the effect of turning the universal rite into a private one, as the person so bathed has entrance only into the congregation(s) so practicing. While the concern for inclusive language is very important both ethically and theologically, as is argued and demonstrated throughout *The Christian Story* series, the departure from the universal formula by individual initiatives is a breach of ecumenical fellowship. Further, the proposed alternatives fail the test of faithfulness to the trinitarian teaching which the formula embodies.[17] For the church universal, "Baptism . . . is administered in the name of the Father, the Son and the Holy Spirit."[18] The meaning of those terms is not taken from patriarchal experience, but from the Story itself, and thus from how the conventional human meanings of "father" or "son" are challenged and transformed by their function in the account of the central chapter, Jesus Christ. That christological norm takes us to the initial meaning of baptism itself.[19]

Incorporation into the Body of Christ

In baptism Christians are brought into union with Christ, with each other, and with the church of every time and place.[20]

The fundamental point being made here under the *BEM* section heading is the entry of the baptized into Christ himself (elsewhere in the same paragraph "union with Christ," and "baptism into Christ"). As "chapter 5" on

17. For a detailed discussion of these issues, see *The Christian Story*, vol. 1, *A Narrative Interpretation of Basic Christian Doctrine*, 3rd edition (Grand Rapids: Eerdmans, 1996), pp. 52-62. A case in point is the theological inadequacy of a proposed alternative, "Creator, Redeemer, Sanctifier." These terms describing the economic Trinity, standing alone as the name of God, host the historic errors of modalism, Arianism, and subordinationism, the Father alone as Creator making the Son a creature, and thus not acknowledging the coinherence and co-equality of the Persons.

18. *BEM*, p. 2.

19. The sequence of the elements of baptism follows the logic of this work, and, in this respect, differs from that of *BEM*, although the number and contents of the elements are the same.

20. *BEM*, p. 3.

the church (in the construal of Christian faith as "the Story") follows "chapter 4" on the Person and Work of Jesus Christ, participation *in* the "benefits of Christ" in the unfolding Story must be where Christ has chosen to continue to be among us, that is, in his Body on earth. To be in the church is to be in Christ. And the initiation into that community is by passage under the waters of baptism.

How evocative and paradoxical this imagery! Bodies are born, yet following the language of Scripture, we are "born of water and the Spirit" (John 3:5). Birth is a coming out from a body, not entry (incorporation) into it; but by baptism we enter, not depart. And yet again, the event of baptism is, beyond its historical pentecostal origins, the birth, ever and again, *of* the Body of Christ itself. Pursuing the birth imagery, collectively and personally, we are in baptism "born again." For the former reason, among others, baptism is properly a public rite, done in the midst of the congregation. In a sense, the people of God are together reborn as water breaks over the new child of God. But here our attention is on entry into Christ by entry into his Body. For all that, one basic meaning of baptism is *participation* in a new environment, veritably in Jesus Christ, *en Christo*, by dint of our entrance into his very own Body on earth. We become members thereof, parts of that new Organism that now inhabits the earth.

Not sufficiently present, though implied, is an aspect of incorporation given high priority since the period of the *BEM* study. Baptism is not only into the church as an organism, but into the ministry of its charisms. If these gifts can be divided between those that keep the Body *alive* and those that keep it *alert* and moving in the world, as heretofore described, then the baptism of 99 percent of the church which does not (yet) have a special ordination to ministry constitutes their commission to ministry. The arms and feet of the Body of Christ are the organs that keep it working and walking in the world over which Christ rules. Again, the ministry of the laity, as that of the pastoral office, is of the *esse* of the church.

Participation in Christ's Death and Burial

When *BEM* lists "participation in Christ" as a heading for a dimension of baptism it associates it specifically with his death and resurrection. Rightly so from Scripture:

Do you not know that all of us who have been baptized into Christ Jesus were baptized into his death? Therefore we have been buried with him by baptism into death, so that, just as Christ was raised from the dead by the glory of the Father, so we too might walk in newness of life. (Rom. 6:3-4)

The turning point in the life of Jesus, the last battle when sin, evil, and death were met in their ugliest reality, and overcome, belongs now not only to Christ but also to the one baptized. To be in him means participation in what happened to him:

To be immersed in the liberating death of Christ where their sins are buried, where the "old Adam" is crucified with Christ, and where the power of sin is broken.[21]

The benefits of the cross, the mercy won by the sacrifice of Christ, are now also those of the baptized. The one receiving the water is cleansed of the sin of the race, and is put on a new track in which the old lord is replaced by a new one. And where there is a repositioning, there is also the offer of power. Life inside the risen Lord means also

being raised here and now to a new life in the power of the resurrection of Jesus Christ. . . .[22]

Christ's death and resurrection bring pardon and power in principle. Baptism into them brings pardon and power in fact. Good Friday and Easter turn the world around, *coram Deo*. In baptism the finished work of Christ on Good Friday and Easter turns the world around *pro me* and *pro nobis*.

To be in the Body of Christ is to be in Christ, and thus to participate in his Person. His Person is inseparable from his Work, his doing from his being. That is why Scripture and the church speak of the second aspect of baptism as "participation in Christ's death and resurrection." As noted earlier, the church is not only a pointer to what Christ has done and will do, but also is a participant in that redeeming work into which we are baptized.

21. *BEM*, p. 2.
22. *BEM*, p. 2.

The Gift of the Spirit

Baptism is a trinitarian event, so signaled by its formula. To be in Christ is to share in the Holy Spirit, the Persons of the triune God being coinherent. Where the second Person is, there also is the third Person, the Spirit being the Spirit of the Son of the Father.

God bestows on all persons the anointing and promise of the Holy Spirit.[23] Where the Spirit is there is new life:

> He saved us, not because of any righteousness that we had done, but according to his mercy, through the water of rebirth and renewal by the Holy Spirit. (Titus 3:5)

As the Holy Spirit was poured out on the apostles at Pentecost from the risen and ruling Lord, so the baptized participates in the descent of the Spirit, just as that same person was joined to the resurrected Lord. And as fresh vitalities were released then by the risen and ascended Lord, the signs of the Spirit, so in baptism the Spirit calls and empowers the baptized to the life of *kerygma, leitourgia, koinonia,* and *diakonia.*

Conversion, Pardoning, and Cleansing

To this point we have spoken of those aspects of baptism that primarily deal with the objective act — what the triune God is doing in the event. Now, in the final two aspects of baptism, the subjective is to the fore. Where the gift is given, a command accompanies it; as baptism places the baptized in new relations to Christ and the church, to the Spirit's gift, to the Father's purposes, baptismal grace calls for a response in kind. Be what you are! You are in Christ, therefore follow him! You have been baptized into his death, therefore take up your cross! You have been turned about, therefore turn around *(metanoiein, epistrophein)*! You have been offered pardon, therefore receive your justification in faith! You have been washed in the waters, therefore be clean! You have been commissioned to ministry, then be what you have been called to be and do! As *BEM* states it simply:

> The New Testament underlines the ethical implications of baptism.[24]

23. *BEM,* p. 2.
24. *BEM,* p. 2.

Ethics here is, in the broadest sense, "doing." That doing may take the form of acts of repentance, faith, or action. "Conversion," again in its broadest sense, is the walk that follows from the face-about in a new direction, a change of space as well as of place.[25]

The Sign of the Kingdom

The kingdom as it finally will be is the reign of God over all, when the purpose of God for life together shall come to be. That eschatological rule, however, is an "already-not yet," a regency that has begun in Jesus Christ. The church, as the Body of Christ on earth, shares in that blessedness to be. Baptism therefore puts one foot into the waters of that wave of the Future. As such, the baptized takes part in a flow that

> embraces the whole of life, extends to all nations, and anticipates the day when every tongue will confess that Jesus Christ is Lord to the glory of God the Father.[26]

The kingdom dimension of baptism summarizes both the gift and demand aspects, as it is a reminder of the call to the baptized to live out their baptism in both Word and deed, in ways that anticipate the way the whole world will some day be. Thus we have moved from that aspect with its focus in the church on earth, to the world in its full compass and the Word in its final fulfillment.

Baptism and Faith

BEM has a special section on the role of faith in the baptismal action. Such takes into account not only the nature of the sacrament itself but also the fact that the ecumenical community includes churches that practice believer's baptism, and yet others who judge such as normative and pedo-baptism as derivative, though the latter remains the standard practice. However construed or practiced, faith and the waters are inseparable, even

---

25. See the writer's "Conversion," in *Word in Deed: Theological Themes in Evangelism* (Grand Rapids: Eerdmans, 1975), pp. 78-105.

26. *BEM*, p. 3.

in the ways that pedobaptism itself is understood — from the belief in presumed faith in the infant to the necessity of vicarious faith in parent, sponsor, and congregation.[27] Thus in all cases,

> The necessity of faith for the reception of the salvation embodied and set forth in baptism is acknowledged by all churches.[28]

However, *BEM* had more than this in mind as indicated in a subsequent sentence:

> Personal commitment is necessary for responsible membership in the church.[29]

How interesting must have been the discussions surrounding the insertion of this sentence, for it clearly moves beyond the substitutionary faith of parent, sponsor, and congregation, and also any supposed inarticulate faith in the infant, to some decision at the age of discretion, confirmatory or initiatory. And not only that but throughout the Christian life:

> Baptism is related not only to momentary experience, but to life-long growth in Christ.[30]

Why the necessity of faith, before, during, or after the pouring of the water or descent into it? Grace, through the baptismal means of grace, is an act of divine outreach. This unconditional welcome is offered to those who do not merit it — the water that flowed from a hill with a cross and Christ's open arms thereon. As in the Galilean Jesus' story that anticipates Calvary, grace does its redemptive work when received in faith, the prodigal running to receive the Father's unconditional embrace. And, of course, the paradox we meet at every turn in Christian teaching is that faith is no work, but itself a gift, the power of the Holy Spirit of the triune God bringing it to be as a response to the grace offered also by the same Spirit.

It has been the charism of the Reformation to bring to the fore the faith alone which meets grace alone. And the left wing of the Reformation has underscored this in its teaching of believer's baptism. We are in the latter's

---

27. *The Christian Story,* vol. 1, pp. 181-83.
28. *BEM,* p. 3.
29. *BEM,* p. 3.
30. *BEM,* p. 4.

debt for that. However, the exclusion of the children of faith from the rite by a focus on our response, however graced, does not do justice to the prevenience of, and catholicity of, its reach represented by baptismal incorporation into the church. The reach goes before our response, signaling the social nature of the church in which one can bear the burden of another. Such larger theological considerations cannot be set aside by a reductionist experientialism and self-righteousness that too often attend the concept of a believers' church, just as much as the erosion of personal responsibility and cultural accommodation imperil the tradition of pedobaptism.

That there is a need for mutual admonition here is apparent in the *BEM* effort to honor the insights of each, acknowledging the importance of the corporate and the individual, the divine initiative and personal response.[31] Historically, recognition of the witness of each has been expressed in the appearance of a rite of dedication of infants in believers' churches, witnessing to the grace that begins at the beginning of the Christian life, and the rite of confirmation at the age of accountability in the pedobaptism tradition. An ecumenical approach will strive for an encompassing journey, one yet to be found for this rite, though mutual affirmation and mutual admonition are first steps toward it.

By baptismal grace entry is made into the church, an encounter there given with its Lord, all by the power of the Spirit and with it a commission to serve the kingdom in ministries in church and world. Grace reaches its ends in saving and serving when it comes home in the response of a graced faith. We close with a cautionary note, that where there is no receiving faith, consequences follow for both the church and the baptized. Karl Barth puts them in the starkest terms:

> The whole teeming, evil humanity of western lands stands under this sign.[32]

The love of God can be hot coals on our heads as well as healing waters (Rom. 12:20). Such realism makes for seriousness in the teaching and learning about the rite before administering and receiving it. So let the gift be celebrated.

---

31. *BEM*, p. 4.

32. Karl Barth, *The Teaching of the Church Regarding Baptism,* trans. E. A. Payne (London: SCM Press, 1949), p. 60.

Eucharist

Under many names — the Lord's Supper, Holy Communion, the Divine Liturgy, the Mass, Eucharist — this "celebration continues as the central act of the Church's worship."[33] Here the Body of Christ is fed, its baptized believers sustained in their Christian life and witness. The bread and wine join the water as acts integral to the being of the church. When the eucharist is understood to "include . . . both word and sacrament,"[34] *kerygma* joined to *leitourgia,* the bread of proclamation to the bread of celebration, then we have in this one rite the singular conjunction of the means of grace that keep the Body of Christ alive.

As in baptism so in the supper, a range of New Testament accounts illustrate and establish the variety of its meanings. They appear in the institution of the eucharist (1 Cor. 11:23-25; Matt. 26:26-29; Mark 14:22-25; Luke 22:14-20) and in reference to its practice in the early life of the Christian community (John 13:1; 6:51-58; Rev. 19:9). Common to them all is the joy and praise to God that

> In the eucharistic meal, in the eating and drinking of the bread and wine, Christ grants communion with himself.[35]

Not once removed, but in "real presence," Jesus comes to the communicant in an "encounter" whose mode is "unique."[36] What he effects here is rich and varied. We examine those gifts under the *BEM* headings, ordered in parallel to the baptismal elements and with an interpretation consonant with *BEM,* yet enlarged in terms of the overall understanding of *leitourgia* here and in our present context.

Communion of the Faithful

As baptism is birth into the family of Christ, so this Meal is nurture necessary for its family members. No feeding, therefore, means no life of, or in,

33. *BEM,* p. 10.

34. *BEM,* p. 10.

35. *BEM,* p. 10. For an effort to show how and why the same Word comes in two ways as visible and audible, see Leonard J. Vander Zee, *Christ, Baptism and the Lord's Supper* (Downers Grove, Ill.: InterVarsity Press, 2004), pp. 135-254.

36. *BEM,* pp. 10, 12.

the Body. The Feast is for the growing family, a growth manifest in varied ways.

The communicant's growth in the faith is inseparable from time at this Table. A "mind of the church" is developing that such nourishment is needed each week. The Lord's Supper is for the Lord's Day. While still not realized in many places, the church universal moves toward this goal. Communion of the Faithful means all the faithful at the Table. It is an event in the life of the church when all the barriers of time and space are breached. While World Communion Sunday has become a yearly calendar event, it is paradigmatic of every celebration, for we are at our Table in every meal with everyone lifting the bread and cup to their mouths. Here is a parable of life together across the divisions of the church, on the one hand, and on the other, of the world's divisions of race, nation, and human differences, and thus a mandate for the church to be in all its relationships what it is *coram Deo* at the Table. The communion of the faithful also crosses the boundary of time, as each celebration brings together the living and the dead, the vast "communion of saints."

Anamnesis, *Communion with Christ*

As baptism brings us into the church, and thus into contact with its Lord, eucharist joins us in continuing living communion with the Head of the Body. This head-to-Head meeting is a matter of remembering, memorial, *anamnesis,* as the service recalls for us the journey of Jesus to its sacrificial center, its vindication and consequence among us, or in BEM's language, "his incarnation, servanthood, ministry, teaching, suffering, sacrifice, resurrection, ascension and sending of the Spirit."[37]

But this is no "head-trip," memorial as only our recollection of what once was. Memorial is the *re-presentation* as well as the visual and verbal presentation of who Christ was and what he did. He *comes to us,* ever and again, in the eating and drinking. Several interpretations of this *real presence* of Christ are worth considering, coming from the Reformed tradition which is sometimes misrepresented as denying such and holding only to a "Zwinglian" view of the eucharist as simply a visual aid to our recollection of Christ's Work. The Mercersburg theologian John Nevin

37. *BEM,* p. 11.

corrects this misunderstanding in his nineteenth-century work, *The Mystical Presence:*

> . . . the sacramental doctrine of the primitive Reformed Church stands inseparably connected with the idea of a living union between believers and Christ, in virtue of which they are incorporated into his very nature, and made to subsist with him by the power of a common life. In full correspondence with this conception of Christian salvation, as a process by which the believer is mystically inserted more and more into the person of Christ, til [becoming] thus at last transformed into his image, it was held that such a real participation of his living person is involved always in the right use of the Lord's Supper.[38]

A contemporary Reformed writer speaks of it this way, citing ecumenical developments:

> One of the more helpful advances in the often thorny discussion of Christ's presence in the sacrament is the more recent movement away from talking about what Christ's "real" presence means to talk about it as Christ's personal presence. Max Thurian describes Christ's presence in the eucharist as a "personal presence which enters into personal relationship with those who believe and receive." The emphasis falls on the personal relationship. A piece of furniture is not *present in a room;* it is *simply there.* People can be very near to one another, even crowded together in one place, in a bus for instance, without being present to one another. Real presence assumes a personal relationship, mind to mind, heart to heart. Still, presence assumes not only a 'spiritual' relationship, but also a physical one: "This personal relationship between people, this being present . . . cannot occur without the mediation of our bodies by which we give each other personal signs of being present."[39]

The journey to "the sacrificial center" of Christ's saving Work raises the question of the relation of the personal real presence of Christ in the

---

38. John Williamson Nevin, *The Mystical Presence* (Philadelphia: J. B. Lippincott & Co., 1846; reprinted by Wipf & Stock Publishers, 2000). Edited by Augustine Thompson, O.P.

39. Vander Zee, *Christ, Baptism and the Lord's Supper,* p. 199. He quotes from Max Thurian, *The Mystery of the Eucharist* (Grand Rapids: Eerdmans, 1984), p. 52.

eucharist to the eucharist *as* a sacrifice. Ecumenical convergence teaching makes it clear that what happens here is not repetition but re-presentation:

> What it was God's will to accomplish in the incarnation, life, death, resurrection and ascension of Christ, God does not repeat. These events neither can be repeated nor prolonged.[40]

The Holy Communion is "the mystical sign of his one offering of himself made once, but of force always."[41] Here is the church's sacrifice of praise and thanksgiving, the eucharist in which he comes to us in nourishing real presence. What this sacrifice of praise and thanksgiving entails is now being widely discussed, ecumenically. At its heart in the tradition of the Reformers is the offering of our own selves. Yet as we partake of the bread and cup and thus are in union with Christ, we participate mysteriously in his own self-offering to the Father, a theme developed fruitfully by Thomas Torrance.[42] For the early Christians living in the hostile environment of the Roman state and emperor worship, participating in Christ's own self-offering at the eucharist might well require a sacrifice in kind.

> Polycarp is tied to the stake in the arena to be burned alive and utters a distinctively worded prayer as this is done, a prayer which is almost certainly intended to echo the kind of prayer he would have used at the eucharist. . . . What matters is that Polycarp or his chronicler or both saw the event of his martyrdom as analogous to the sacrament.[43]

Invocation of the Spirit

As in baptism, so in eucharist, we have to do with the work of the triune God. Christ is present by the Spirit of the Son who makes things happen.

---

40. *BEM,* pp. 11-12.

41. "Preparatory Service," *The Hymnal,* p. 18.

42. For a discussion of the current ecumenical dialogue on the dimension of sacrifice in the eucharist, see Vander Zee, *Christ, Baptism and the Lord's Supper,* pp. 204-10.

43. Rowan Williams, *Why Study the Past? The Quest for the Historical Church* (Grand Rapids: Eerdmans, 2005), p. 36. For what this might mean in contemporary terms see Marva J. Dawn, *Power, Weakness, and the Tabernacling of God* (Grand Rapids: Eerdmans, 2001).

The Spirit makes the crucified and risen Christ really present to us in the eucharistic meal.[44]

However expressed liturgically, the Holy Spirit is asked to do this deed, and does it.

The conjunction of Christ and the Spirit, the companionship of the second and third Persons, is necessary for the Meal to be what it is. Thus the words of Jesus are repeated in the service itself, and the power to make them efficacious is deployed to make real the assertion that "This is my body, this is my blood":

> It is in virtue of the living word of Christ and the power of the Holy Spirit that the bread and wine become the sacramental signs of Christ's body and blood.[45]

In most traditions, and in ecumenical trends, the *epiclesis*, the verbal invocation, is integral to the act.[46]

Thanksgiving to the Father

The Father is always there with the Son and Spirit in the triune God's sacramental meal. Such is signaled in the very name, for it is an occasion of the

> great thanksgiving to the Father for everything accomplished in creation, redemption and sanctification, for everything accomplished by God now in the Church and in the world in spite of the sins of human beings, for everything God will accomplish in bringing the Kingdom to fulfillment.[47]

The eucharistic prayer lines out the acts in the drama, the chapters in the Grand Narrative, giving praise to the Father for the missions accomplished, accomplishing and to be accomplished, so done by the One God and co-indwelling Persons. Thus *kerygma* is again bonded to *leitourgia*,

---

44. *BEM*, p. 13.

45. *BEM*, p. 13.

46. Albeit argued otherwise by some within the Lutheran tradition, the narrative and full liturgy considered an invocation in itself.

47. *BEM*, p. 10.

here the prayed Word as background for what is said in the preached Word at the eucharistic table.

Meal of the Kingdom

Where there is gift, there is command. Where there is Christ present and past, the eternal Lord will be there as Future as well. The meal of Christ is eschatological in every sense — in time, place, and beyond time, with claims to make according to the expectations of what will be. As noted earlier in our discussion of the relation of eschatology to ecclesiology,

> the eucharist opens up the vision of the divine rule which has been promised as the final renewal of creation, and is a foretaste of it.[48]

Thus the meal of the kingdom is at the very center of the continuity between what is in the life of the church and what will be in the End.

This has vast implications for the practice of the church:

> Signs of this renewal are present wherever the grace of God is manifest and human beings work for justice, love and peace. . . .[49]

Partaking of the body and blood of Christ is a pledge to care for bodies broken in a world short of the reign of God, weeping over the blood spilled in a world of war, hurt, and hate, or a nature fallen and fearsome in its destructive state short of the *eschaton*,[50] and a vow to work to set up signs to the peaceable kingdom to come. Here, as before, the imperatives are joined to the indicatives of eucharist. Ethical commission is joined to the Great Commission for those who share now in the meal of a kingdom in which every knee is bowed to Christ the Lord.

> The eucharistic community is nourished and strengthened for confessing by word and action the Lord Jesus who gave his life for the

48. *BEM*, p. 14.

49. *BEM*, p. 14.

50. For a profound wrestle with the issue of theodicy as it expresses itself in the fallenness of nature, so present with us in disasters of the early twenty-first century, see David Bentley Hart, *The Doors of the Sea: Where Was God in the Tsunami?* (Grand Rapids: Eerdmans, 2005).

world. As it becomes one people, sharing the meal of the one Lord, the eucharistic assembly must be concerned for gathering those also who are present beyond its visible limits, because Christ invited to his feast all for whom he died.[51]

Evangelization too is part and parcel of the charge given by the living Lord at his Table, telling the Story as the outcome of celebrating it. Here baptism is linked again to eucharist, for the eucharistic community is enjoined to invite all to the Table by joining the family through the confession and cleansing of the Bath.

As indicated earlier, a current move is being made in some quarters to sever baptism from eucharist, as Christian hospitality is seen to demand an "open Table." The question is put this way by James Farwell in *The Anglican Review:*

> On any given Sunday should "seekers," those "passing through," unbaptized guests or family members of parishioners, the spiritually curious, or even people of other religions be invited and encouraged to receive the consecrated bread and wine of the eucharist?[52]

Although a critic of the proposal, he goes on to describe its rationale:

> If the meal ministry of Jesus incarnated his vision of the kingdom of God, then ours ought to do the same. Making "baptism" the door to the table is an exclusionary rule, suggesting that one must enter the circle of holiness before one can commune with the faithful. In short, if Jesus was hospitable to all, then we should be hospitable to all. If God is open to all, then our table should be open to all.[53]

Evaluating this proposal from the point of view of this ecclesiology entails an examination of both its ecumenical consequences and its theological import. First, the ecumenical implications.

The linkage of Bath and Meal is a refrain in the corporate ecumenical agreements dealing with sacraments. So *BEM:*

---

51. *BEM,* p. 15.

52. James Farwell, "Baptism, Eucharist, and the Hospitality of Jesus: On the Practice of 'Open Communion,'" *The Anglican Review* 86, no. 2 (Spring 2004): 216.

53. Farwell, "Baptism, Eucharist, and the Hospitality of Jesus," p. 219.

Christ commanded his disciples thus to remember and encounter him in this sacramental meal as the continuing people of God until his return. . . . The eucharist is essentially the sacrament of the gift which God makes to us in Christ through the Holy Spirit. Every Christian receives this gift of salvation through communion in the body and blood of Christ . . . each baptized member of the body of Christ receives in the eucharist the assurance of the forgiveness of sins . . . and the pledge of eternal life.[54]

Echoing the words about the eucharist as the meal for Christ's "disciples," "every Christian," "each baptized member," the Lutheran-Episcopal Agreement declares:

We affirm the mystery of the New Birth in Christ by water and the Spirit. Holy Baptism, duly administered with water and in the name of the Father, and of the Son and of the Holy Spirit, and understood as God's action of adoption, initiates into the Body of Christ and (in principle at least) gives access to the Holy Eucharist and the reception of Holy Communion.[55]

Or again, the Anglican-Orthodox "agreed statement on the eucharist":

Baptism in the name of the Father and of the Son and of the Holy Spirit, as many ecumenical statements, including our own on Christian initiation . . . , have affirmed, is the unrepeatable means of our rebirth and incorporation into the body of Christ through the action of the Holy Spirit. It is in the Eucharist that this new life in Christ is nourished and strengthened by the same action of the Holy Spirit.[56]

Echoing the foregoing is the Lutheran-Reformed 1997 "Formula of Agreement," the *COCU* and CUIC (Churches Uniting in Christ). The FOA cites *Marburg Revisted* and *Invitation to Action* as presupposition for the sacramental teaching of its participants, the UCC and RCA included. Both echo

---

54. "Eucharist," *Baptism, Eucharist and Ministry* (Geneva: WCC Publications, 1982), p. 10.

55. "Lutheran-Episcopal Dialogue: Progress Report," in Joseph A. Burgess and Jeffrey Gros, FSC, *Growing Consensus: Church Dialogues in the United States, 1962-1991* (New York: Paulist Press, 1995), p. 176.

56. "Agreed Statement on the Eucharist," *Growing Consensus*, p. 343.

BEM and *Invitation to Action,* specifically citing that document as its premise, "communion of the faithful" being one of its five themes, with the latter's joint statement on the Lord's Supper affirming that "Holy Communion richly nourishes us in our devotion to a life of faithful discipleship. . . ." Baptism initiates into discipleship and Holy Communion nourishes the disciple. *The COCU Consensus* puts the same thing this way in speaking about confirmation "as an effective sign of continuing and growing incorporation into the life of Christ (Eph 4:13-16), of which Baptism is the foundation and the Eucharist is the regular renewal."

The long tradition of the church is summed up this way in the *Catechism of the Catholic Church,* albeit with its distinctive emphasis of sacrifice:

> The holy Eucharist completes Christian initiation. Those who have been raised to the dignity of the royal priesthood by Baptism and configured more deeply by Confirmation participate with the whole community in the Lord's own sacrifice by means of the Eucharist.[57]

Jane Rogers Vann, noting the collision between historic and ecumenical teaching on the Bath-Meal sequence, observes,

> In an age of instant gratification, the idea of withholding anything at all, from simple treats to extraordinary privileges (and their attendant responsibilities), is quite unusual. This culture of indulgence makes the church's insistence on the traditional sequence of baptism and Eucharist seem harsh.[58]

As important as the ecumenical testimony is, the linkage of Bath and Meal is based on the nature of the sacrament itself (inherent, of course, in the ecumenical consensus). As the eucharist is a "union with Christ," a

---

57. "The Sacrament of the Eucharist," Article 3, paragraph 1322, *Catechism of the Catholic Church,* English translation (Liguori, Mo.: Liguori Publications, 1994), p. 334. But is this an ecumenical consensus? Some Reformed churches in Europe are exploring the "open table" but surrounding it with many qualifications. Methodists in the United States have considered it as an option, albeit following up the communicant's initial participation with counsel on the necessity of baptism for continuing participation in the eucharist. However, the precedent for this, or even the unrestricted "open Table," as a "converting ordinance" espoused by John Wesley, is unsubstantiated, for no one has been able to find a recorded case of Wesley knowingly admitting an unbaptized person to communion.

58. Jane Rogers Vann, "As I See It Today: The Blessing of a Eucharistic Blessing," Union Theological Seminary & Presbyterian School of Christian Education pamphlet.

meeting with his "real personal Presence," it requires a faith in, love for, and commitment to the One who comes to his own. Hence the classical admonishments, and preparations required for approach to this holy Meal, the "discernment" entailed in a "worthy" act of eating and drinking (1 Cor. 11:27-32). So we move to the larger question of the relation of the faith of the communicant, confessing Christian or otherwise, to the eucharist.

Eucharist and Faith

Why confession of sin, assurance of pardon, and confession of faith before Mealtime in the church ecumenical? Why in some traditions a full-scale preparatory service?[59] As with baptism, so with eucharist, reception of the grace offered in these means is by faith alone. The Christ who is present with open arms to feed those gathered at the Table wants open mouths and hearts. Faith is the movement that meets the bread and cup offered. With such a receiving, grace does its nourishing work building up the Body and the believer.

As in baptism, so in eucharist, where there is no faith, consequences follow. Paul spoke of such to the Corinthian church:

> Whoever, therefore, eats the bread and drinks the cup of the Lord in an unworthy manner will be answerable for the body and blood of the Lord. Examine yourselves and only then eat of the bread and drink of the cup. For all who eat and drink without discerning the body, eat and drink judgment against themselves. For this reason many of you are weak and ill, and some have died. (1 Cor. 11:27-30)

Tough talk, indeed, but fitting to the tough love of God. If this sacrament, like that of baptism, is what we say it is, a meeting, firsthand, with Jesus

---

59. So the words of the Preparatory Service for Holy Communion in *The Hymnal* of the Evangelical and Reformed Church, later to become part of the United Church of Christ: "Being of such a sacred nature it is plain that the Table of the Lord can be rightly approached only by those who are of truly devout, repentant and believing mind. These holy mysteries are not for the worldly, the irreverent or the indifferent. All who are impenitent, unbelieving and who refuse to obey the Gospel of our Lord Christ have no right to partake of this Table." *The Hymnal,* p. 28.

Christ, then we have to do with the Christ of accountability as well as the Christ of acceptance, no indulgent deity, but one whose gift is accompanied by command.

Where the eucharist has been transformed into the extension of a postmodern normlessness traveling under the ideology of "inclusivity" and justified by the blessed word of "hospitality," standards of discipline disappear. Thus into our worship enters the kind of theology that H. Richard Niebuhr famously characterized in the notable sentence: "A God without wrath brought [humans] without sin into a kingdom without judgment through the ministrations of a Christ without a cross."[60]

Worship in Its Width

There is "a wideness in God's mercy" and a width in the ways of prayer. The spectrum has been characterized with acronyms — for example, ACTS as adoration, confession, thanksgiving, supplication; or ACTION — adoration, confession, thanksgiving, intercession, offering of oneself as needy (petition), naming the Holy Name; or the "five fingers" in each praying hand — adoration, confession, intercession, petition, thanksgiving; following the model of Isaiah 6:1-18 — adoration, confession, thanksgiving, hearing the call, commitment.[61]

Adoration

Notable in each sequence is the constancy of "adoration" as the first movement of our spirit in the life of prayer. How different this is from popular understandings of prayer that focus on the self's primacy, as in prayer conceived only as petition to meet our needs. Not so in classical prayer where the first thought is of God. So the beginning of the Lord's own prayer,

---

60. H. Richard Niebuhr, *The Kingdom of God in America* (New York: Harper & Bros., 1937; Harper Torchbooks, 1959), p. 193.

61. For some of these leads, thanks go to Willis Elliott who edited the *Fellowship of Prayer* booklets for many years. See also the articles on the subject in *The Westminster Dictionary of Christian Spirituality* and *The New Westminster Dictionary of Liturgy and Worship*. As noted, writer and spouse used the Isaiah 6 framework, with enlargements in *Christian Basics*, pp. 101-12.

"Our Father who art in Heaven, hallowed by thy name. . . ." "Thy" not "my" name is in the place of honor in Christian prayer. God and the divine glory constitute the point of orientation. Eucharist, as praise and thanksgiving to God, is prayer writ large; and all other prayer, derivative therefrom, is the same, writ small. Personal piety and corporate worship other than the eucharist strike this note, first and foremost.

Praise to God for what? The question can be answered by reference to a typical hymnbook, which places at the outset just this primary note variously identified as praise, adoration, or thanksgiving. Take two of the most familiar hymns of praise and adoration that appear in this way: "Holy, Holy, Holy" and "Come Thou Almighty King." Both are trinitarian hymns. The first is praise for the triune God, simply for being the triune God as in Isaiah's exultation with the cherubim and seraphim around the throne rejoicing, to the visions of the book of Revelation with saints around the throne casting down their crowns before the blessed Trinity, "perfect in power, love and purity." The second looks to the deeds of the triune God, the great drama in which we dwell on the majestic Father, the incarnate Word, and the Holy Comforter, each in their missions in the history of God. Again, the eucharist is seen as a backdrop for one of its meanings as in "thanksgiving to the Father," in which the divine deeds are remembered — from creation to Christ to consummation. Praise is the signature of Christian prayer, the adoration of God for the sake of the Trinity's very being, and thanksgiving for what God has done, is doing, and will do among and for us.

It is worth comparing these great refrains in primal Christian prayer as praise to the triune God for the divine being and doing to what is called in popular idiom "praise music." Here is a stanza from a popular "praise song":

God is good. God is good
God is good. He's so good to me
I'll do his will. He loves me so
He answers prayer.

And from another:

I stand before you king of my heart
I know you see me, I'm your work of art

You are the Creator, the God above,
the one true almighty whose language is love
Glory, glory, show me your glory,
Glory, glory, show me your glory. . . .

The contrast with the two earlier cited hymns of praise is striking. Praise songs of this kind make no mention of the triune God. Indeed, while described as praise to God, the focus is not theocentric but anthropocentric. In the first case, the rationale for praise is what God does for me: "He's so good to me. . . . He loves me so, He answers prayer." Yes, on all counts, but where is the Grand Narrative of what God does for the whole world, and where is the love of God for God's own sake, not for self-service? In the second song, while the refrain is rightly the glory of God, the verses are petitionary prayer, again centered on "I, me, and mine" with thirty-three allusions to the same in the song, the request being to show God's glory to the one praying, rather than praise for what is manifest in the being and doing of the triune God. Quite apart from the question of the quality of the music, the doctrine embedded in these modern praise songs is shallow when compared to the doctrinal solidities of the classical hymnody of praise and adoration.

A steady diet of praise songs and their kin, now making their way into standard-brand congregations seeking "success," is reason to be concerned about the future of genuine praise in the congregations of tomorrow.

While the anthropocentrism of much current praise music is here to the fore, comparable obeisance to cultural trends can be seen in hymnody of mainline churches where "inclusivity" is often understood to exclude, ironically, the same Trinity that is missing in popular praise music.[62]

To the second band in the spectrum, we now turn — confession.

Confession

Again, following the recurring sequence, prayer as confession of sin is the next step on the journey.

---

62. So the critique found in Richard Christensen, ed., *How Shall We Sing the Lord's Song?: An Assessment of the New Century Hymnal* (Allison Park, Pa.: Pickwick Publications, 1997).

"Woe is me, I am lost, for I am a man of unclean lips and I live among a people of unclean lips. . . ." (Isaiah 6:3)

Why this order? As the prophet measures himself against the glory of God, so the Christian takes stock of the self and the church before the glory "in the face of Jesus Christ" (2 Cor. 5:6), and the contrast drives us to our knees.

The praise that ascends to the triune God looks back down on where we are. God is a Loving Life Together and we are perpetrators of discord, strife, and war. All Persons are total in their Self-giving and out-going to the Others. We are self-absorbed and incurved (Luther — *incurvatus ad se*). The immanent inner-trinitarian being of infinite Love we know from the works of the triune God *ad extra,* creating, reconciling, sanctifying. And it is through the lens at the Center that we see the Story in its fullness.

Various traditions have described the encounter with the divine glory differently. Martin Luther called the awakening to our sin, graphically, the "thunderbolt of God," this "second office of the law" (its "theological use," alongside its "civil use" and the often disputed third, pedagogical use).[63] This is the lightning of God's love which exposes us for who we are, and strikes us down to our knees in prayerful penitence. Cornelius Plantinga identifies the bolt's target as "the hard heart and the stiff neck" of the imperial self, our moral lawlessness and spiritual faithlessness.[64] What else then in worship than the movement from praise of God's glory to the confession of our sin:

Almighty and most merciful God, we have erred and strayed from your ways like lost sheep. We have followed too much the devices and desires of our own hearts. . . .

The believer confesses that the first of the things we must know about ourselves to live and die in the comfort of the gospel is "the greatness of my sin and wretchedness."[65]

63. Interestingly, Calvin, for whom the sovereignty and glory of God were a defining accent, makes it the first use of the law.

64. For a searching inquiry into this subject, see Cornelius Plantinga, Jr., *Not the Way It's Supposed to Be: A Breviary of Sin* (Grand Rapids: Eerdmans, 1995). On the theological use of the law see the writer's "The Thunderbolt of God" in the online *Journal of Lutheran Ethics,* October 2003.

65. Heidelberg Catechism, Question 2.

The movement of the soul's prayer parallels the track of the Great Drama itself. Scene 2 in Act I is the account of the fall that follows the overflowing love of God for us in the mighty deed of creation. The difference is that we now know what we have done and to whom to say, pastor and people responsively,

> Lord, have mercy upon us,
> Christ, have mercy upon us,
> Lord, have mercy upon us.

As the music of worship lives out the phases of prayer, how important that section of the hymnal! So the sequence is expressed in the great hymn:

> Saviour when in dust to Thee, Low we bow the adoring knee.
> When repentant to the skies, scarce we lift our weeping eyes. . . .[66]

And at that lower depth, Luther's own heartfelt sung words:

> Out of the depths I cry to thee, Lord,
> Hear me, I implore thee,
> Bend down thy gracious ear to me.
> Let my prayer come before thee.[67]

And we must ask of the audience for the popular music urged upon the pastor, "Is there a like word of confession to be heard in its verses? How can genuine praise of God not be inextricable from penitence before God?"

Thanksgiving

The natural movement of Christian prayer, as presented by the acronyms, instructions in piety, and movement of the liturgy, is to gratitude. For what? Already, we have addressed the question: for that Act in the Great Drama that speaks directly to our state of sin. We hear the Word about it in the assurance of pardon and absolution, and our prayerful response is

---

66. Robert Grant, "Saviour When in Dust to Thee," *The Hymnal* (St. Louis: Eden Publishing House, 1947), 219.
67. Martin Luther, "Out of the Depths I Cry to Thee," *The Hymnal*, 210.

Lord, open thou my lips
And my mouth shall show forth thy praise!

Here, praise and thanksgiving recur, but now not to the Trinity as such, as in the first step on the journey, but to the singular deed done by the triune God in the Person and Work of Jesus Christ. We thank God for "how I am freed from all my sins and their wretched consequences and [say] what gratitude I owe to God for such a redemption."[68]

Prayer of focal gratitude takes us to the turning point of the Christian Story. God has stepped in to deal directly with the demons — preeminently our sin, derivatively and accompanyingly the power of evil that fells nature, as well — and the death of estrangement from God and the divine purposes that lies threateningly over all creation. They have met their match! On the cross and at the empty tomb, the victory has been won. In the economy of the triune God, the Father sent the Son who in the power of the Holy Spirit did the deed. Who cannot shout for joy to God! And so we do in the liturgy, as in an older language:

> Glory be to God on High, and on earth, peace, good will to all. We praise thee, we bless thee, we worship thee, we glorify thee, we give thanks to thee for thy great glory: O Lord God, heavenly King, God the Father Almighty. O Lord, the only begotten Son, Jesus Christ; O Lord God, Lamb of God, Son of the Father, that taketh away the sins of the world, have mercy upon us. Thou that takest away the sins of the world, receive our prayer. Thou that sittest at the right hand of God the Father, have mercy upon us. For thou alone art holy; thou only art the Lord; thou only, O Christ, with the Holy Ghost, art most high in the glory of God the Father. Amen.[69]

The music of prayer in the Great Tradition strikes all the notes in the chorus of trinitarian faith here too at the turning point in the Tale of God. May music that purports to be praise, of either the gospel writ large or writ small — the Grand Drama in its entirety, or its central Act — follow the lead of the Gloria in Excelsis.

There is this Great Thanksgiving for the deed of God in Christ, and

---

68. Heidelberg Catechism, Question 2.
69. "Canticle of God's Glory (Gloria in Excelsis)," *The United Methodist Hymnal* (Nashville: United Methodist Publishing House), p. 82.

there are derivative gratitudes for the bounties of the God revealed in Christ. The prayers of thanksgiving are many and varied. "Thanksgiving" as a season reminds us of one so meaningful to days when harvest meant life and death, even as they still do in drought-ridden parts of this world. Thanksgiving for the work of Providence in history as well as nature, when tribulations are not our lot and peace comes and justice does roll down as the waters. And in our personal history when we see the working of a Providence closer to home. But then why so much misery at other times and places, and among other persons or ourselves? Theodicy, the "problem of evil," tracks our talk of the graces in nature and history — public and personal. Elsewhere in this series we have spoken of the misconception of God as an instant and everywhere despot, a notion forgetful of the suffering God who works by persuasion not force in this fallen world, with much "not the way it's supposed to be," yet who *will be* "all in all" at time's closure.[70] Until then we are grateful for the signs of that final victory, and so "Rejoice in the Lord always; again I say rejoice" (Phil. 4:4).

Supplication

"I will do whatever you ask in my name . . ." (John 14:13). What a promise! Yet how could such be? Unnumbered things *have* been asked "in Jesus' name" which have not come to be.

To ask "in Jesus' name" means to ask in conformity with who he was and is, and to align with the divine purposes. Did the "unanswered" prayers so cohere? Could answers have been given that did cohere but were not those that fit our definition and expectation? Do we honor the difference between mystery and magic in our prayers, the one assuming that we can control deity and the other trusting in the divine sovereignty with its wisdom not our own? Christian "asking" in Jesus' name is different in kind from "religion" that seeks to use the divine for human purposes however meritorious.[71]

For all the right qualifications of this sort with which we must sur-

---

70. *The Christian Story,* vol. 1, pp. 240-45.

71. For the writer's early struggle with the role of "religion" in Christian faith in the light of Bonhoeffer's critique of the "God-of-the-gaps," see *Humiliation and Celebration: Post-Radical Themes in Doctrine, Morals and Mission* (New York: Sheed & Ward, 1969), pp. 127-38.

round it, supplication is in the arsenal of prayer. Indeed, it is a weapon in the war against the Evil One. As co-belligerents with Jesus in his struggle between the times of his ascension and second advent, his counsel to ask and promise to help in the battle against sin, evil, and death are to be believed. The act of supplication to which we are called, like that within the paradigmatic entreaties in the book of Psalms and in Jesus' own prayers to the Father, is twofold: intercession and petition. We ask the triune God in Jesus' name, and thus in conformity to his will and purposes, to help others and to help ourselves. To listen to the request for such is the growing practice of pastors who invite parishioners to express their joys and concerns in public worship. Such a practice reminds us that those we serve have this kind of prayer much on their minds and in their hearts, concerns far outweighing thanksgivings (the need for pedagogy on prayer thus signaled, indeed, the thanksgivings of the derivative sort just discussed, spoken out of the center of gratitude for who God is and what God has done in Christ). Notable also in the congregation's positive response to the invitation to supplication is the rejection of the universe as a closed system whose "natural laws" shield it from its Maker's entrance, ever and again, to support the healing and hope in this world for the *shalom* for which it is intended by the God who is *Shalom*.

As Intercession

As Christ is "the man for others" (Dietrich Bonhoeffer), so the supplications as well as the deeds of his followers are "for others." Intercessory prayer is a Samaritan intervention for the victims on the world's Jericho roads. Along with whatever we can do to bind up wounds with our hands, we do as well with our hearts. See the cascade of entreaties in any church's "Book of Worship": for all sorts and conditions . . . for the rulers of all lands and the peace of the world . . . for those who suffer heavy affliction, are in want, under oppression, in hunger . . . for those in sore temptations, sorrow, dying, bereavement (and in some, for the dead), for protection from earthquake, fire, and flood, for those who do not know the gospel and those who are its emissaries, for the church universal. . . .

Intercession is in specifics as well as in generalities: this ruler of this land, the present state of this country, the ending of this war, this child with hungry eyes and mouth, this person fractured by injustice, this tempted spirit, this sick or dying body, this dead soul, these people whose homes are engulfed by fire and flood, this person who needs to hear the gospel, this missionary, this congregation . . .

As Petition

"Make me a captive, Lord," "Lord, speak to me," "Have thine own way, Lord," "Abide with me," "Lord have mercy, Christ have mercy, Lord have mercy," "Be present at our table, Lord," "Lord make me an instrument of your peace. . . ." These hymnic, liturgical, and classical prayers point to where Christian petition begins. We supplicate God for ourselves about *the things of God.* Christian petition begins by asking God to "have thine own way" with us, whatever that requires on this stage of our pilgrimage: supporting by grace the faith alone that saves and thus mercy on believers that continue *simul iustus et peccator,* strengthening us to resist the tempter's power. Speaking to us the Word we need, being with us at the Table/table, emboldening and illuminating us for faithful service, consoling us at the close of our journey.

Not anywhere in the above list are the conventional askings. They do belong, but not first and foremost, else the theocentricity of prayer departs into anthropocentric byways. Yes, ask for the human rudiments — food, clothing, and shelter, healing of our diseases, survival in the face of earthquake, hurricane, flood, and fire, protection from the enemy's advances, the criminal's attacks, the bully's fists, life in the face of death. How else can the first petitions be answered if the second are not? We do not live by bread alone, but we do live in the body by bread so that we can live in the soul by faith alone and serve in love both the body and soul of the "other."

Petition has its model, again, in the Lord's own prayer. We note that there the "I, me, mine" that are so much part of conventional petition are replaced by plural pronouns, thus marking the fullness of supplication. So in both petitions of the soul and of the body, it is both "be with *us* in the time of temptation" and "give *us* this day our daily bread." And in dealing with the Power that is the source of one and the foe of the other, it is again a blend of petition and intercession: "deliver *us* from Evil."

And the final note on supplication from the Lord's own prayer. As we honor the divine sovereignty in praise and adoration at the peak point of prayer, so in lesser regions, the sovereignty of God is to be remembered. Our wills are to the fore in petition and intercession, but it is Another's will that finally prevails, a divine will on the particulars of supplicatory prayer known to God alone. Thus from the "Our Father" we always add: in thought if not word, thy will be done on earth, not ours, even as it is and will be done in heaven.

Catholicity

The "Vincentian canon" holds catholicity to be "what is believed by everyone, always and everywhere." Much disputed as a description of what is the case, or about the conditions that make it the case, we have taken the position in this work that this canon can be stated in the idiom of *leitourgia*, as "what is practiced by everyone, always and everywhere." That is, with the exceptions duly noted, as applies to the very rule,[72] the universal mark of the catholicity is the worship of the church, with baptism and eucharist at its center, eucharist understood as proclamation as well as celebration. Thus, again, where the Word is rightly preached and the sacraments rightly administered, there is the church always and everywhere of everyone, no matter the label. Where the church, in this sense, is catholic, it exists; where no such mark is found, it does not.

The New Testament trinitarian images summarize the nature of the church's catholicity in both its human and divine dimensions.

The church catholic is where the people of the triune God raise their voices in praise and prayer. While our adoration, confession, thanksgiving, intercessions, petitions, and commitments are faltering and flawed, the divine Ear is always open to the pentecostal *people of God.*

The church catholic exists as the *Body of Christ* baptizes at its members' beginnings and celebrates at its eucharistic heart. While the baptized may not live out their death and resurrection as intended, and are not worthy to come to the Table on their own merits, the promise of the Christ is to be believed — to be healingly present in the eating and drinking for those who come in penitence and faith.

The catholicity of the church is assured when the *Temple of the Spirit* is built among us. While this house is not yet made without human hands, and thus subject to the damages that can come from our craft, the font and

---

72. The Society of Friends arguably so, but also the exceptions made to the universality of baptism by the Roman Catholic Church, as in the alternative in exceptional cases of baptism by intention and by martyrdom.

table are the signs of a Spirit stronger than our weaknesses, securing the foundations and center of the Temple.

As in the Acts account of the first church, *leitourgia* manifested itself to those without as well as within the congregation. The focus in this chapter has been on the nurture of the church through sacrament, praise, and prayer. Yet now as then, the worshiping people of God strain toward mission, as in the very claims of baptism and eucharist. Beyond those we must ask how the liturgical life can be missionary as well as nurturing. The medieval church did it through porch plays for the whole community and congregations today through Palm Sunday parades and Easter sunrise services. Yet the outreach remains a challenge to the liturgical imagination yet to be fully engaged in our time and place.

CHAPTER 6

Diakonia: *Service and Sanctity*

"The holy," in standard interpretation, has to do with the "sacred" things of God.[1] Rudolf Otto explored that meaning in his classical work, *The Idea of the Holy.*[2] John Webster recently has placed it rightly in its trinitarian context in his extended reflection on "holiness."[3] This understanding of the term continues in Christian usage, both objectively and subjectively. On the one hand, the holy has to do with the presence of God in our midst, and the other, our response in kind to that presence, both in explicit acts of piety and also in "holy living" understood as righteous behavior. As we relate the holiness of the church to the signs of the Holy Spirit in the church, the holy understood as the divine presence is fundamental to its meaning as an attribute of the church. How that *objective* holiness is understood will be explored here. However, as the sign of the Spirit that appeared *subjectively* in the primitive congregation, in contrast to other signs of the Spirit, "righteous behavior" as holy living in conduct

1. See Rowan Williams, *Why Study the Past? The Quest for the Historical Church* (Grand Rapids: Eerdmans, 2005), pp. 32-40 for this familiar rendition of the terminology.

2. Rudolf Otto, *The Idea of the Holy: An Inquiry into the Non-Rational Factor in the Idea of the Divine and Its Relation to the Rational,* trans. John W. Harvey (Oxford: Oxford University Press, 1957).

3. John Webster, *Holiness* (Grand Rapids: Eerdmans, 2003), p. 4 and "Introduction," pp. 1-7.

toward the neighbor in need comes dramatically to the fore. Here the sign of holiness is how human beings in dire circumstances receive the caring and sharing that a "holy community" cannot fail to be and do. It is in this sense that we shall understand this sign of the Spirit in the first congregation, and how we shall here interpret the attribute of sanctity in its visible form.[4] Of course, such holy living is related to sanctity in its invisible form, the holiness granted by grace *coram Deo* even when the works of righteousness are not immediately present.

Rowan Williams observes that for the first Christians the manifestation of "sacred power" — holiness as the fruits by which this particular people were known — meant radical distinction from the practices of the world around them, and therefore life as "resident aliens." Citing the *Letter to Diognetus,* he comments:

> Christians behave differently — a frequent theme in second century literature; they forswear promiscuity, infanticide (including abortion), fraud and violence, and of course in the most counter-cultural witness of all, they will face death for their commitment.[5]

The paradigmatic church in its earliest expression was inconceivable apart from behavioral evidence before the world of its status before God. In that respect, the second-century Christian community was showing the diaconal sign of the Spirit.

Dramatic examples of diaconal behavior came in many and varied ways, as in the earlier-cited care for bodies in need:

> All who believed had all things in common; they would sell their possessions and goods and distribute the proceeds to all as any had need. . . . But Peter said, "I have no silver or gold, but what I have, I give you; in the name of Jesus Christ of Nazareth, stand up and walk." (Acts 2:44-45; 3:6)

The sanctity demonstrated in radical fashion by the Christian communities of the early centuries poses serious questions to us in the church to-

---

4. In contrast, for example, to Webster's treatment of "holiness" in its responsive dimension, which gives attention principally to what has been described here as the visibilities of *kerygma* and *leitourgia*, devoting only two pages to *diakonia* (pp. 96-98) and that in relationship to the "holiness of the Christian" not the "holiness of the church." Webster, *Holiness.*

5. Williams, *Why Study the Past?* p. 37.

day, and has done so, as well, in the whole sweep of Christian history since New Testament times. How much comparable evidence of this kind of visible holiness can be found — whether it be the New Testament sharing of goods, the miraculous healing of bodies, or the sharp juxtaposition of Christian behavior to cultural practices and willingness to die for such? Is there a Word here for the church everywhere and always?

To answer this question, we return to a subject taken up in Volume 2 of this series: How are biblical texts to be interpreted? A case was made for the fourfold sense of Scripture as common, critical, canonical, and contextual.[6]

Interpreting the Text

Common-sense-wise, these are stories of a church empowered for total sharing, one with the other, and for miracle-working. Common sense includes also the community's reading over time, which expanded the meaning to include the ordinary as well as the extraordinary. In the latter case, we see these early signs replicated in utopian Christian communities and in orders within the church catholic. Again, miraculous healings are expected as part of pentecostal practice, and can be found in the answered prayer of believers everywhere.[7] Yet throughout Christian history, the wisdom of the Body of Christ has extended the circumference of meaning to

---

6. Fackre, *The Christian Story*, vol. 2, *Authority: Scripture in the Church for the World* (Grand Rapids: Eerdmans, 1987), pp. 158-210.

7. A 2006 report of a study by Harvard researchers announced its finding that there was no correlation between intercessions for the sick and healing from surgery, known or unknown by the ones for whom prayers were being offered. For a tongue-in-cheek response by a wise pastor, see Martin Copenhaver, "Let Us Not Pray," *The Christian Century* 123, no. 9 (May 2, 2006): 9.

Of course intercession is only one kind of prayer and no statistical research can touch the reality of thanksgiving, praise, confession. . . . And Christians do not believe intercession and petition are magic, the manipulation of the sovereign and free God, or that believers are exempt from the fall of nature with its cancers and tsunamis. But what the researchers can't measure is how intercessions are connected with the way the ones prayed for are empowered to deal with the tribulation. They are. And that the good and all-powerful God who knows firsthand on the cross about the worst of suffering is not bound to some principle never to heal, any more than being captive to a researcher's statistics. So the Scripture's tales of Christ the healer. And the God who planted in our hearts the confidence that ultimately, if not penultimately, "all will be well, all will be well."

include a wider range of ministry to and with the sick, the poor, and the broken. To this wider meaning we shall return in further senses of these Scriptures. For now we observe that the name of the book in which these accounts appear is "Acts," underscoring Christian behavior — the *acts* of the apostles, not only their talks.[8] "Talk" will not be here demeaned, the too-facile charge of "activists." The *language* of the apostles was inextricable from the very being of the church, having to do with the Word preached and celebrated in worship, the prayers lifted, the *kerygma* and *leitourgia* earlier explored. But the church in its fullness entails a third sign, *diakonia*, the Word done, as well as the Word proclaimed and celebrated, a ministration to human need in its earthiest form, the care of persons in their bodies as well as souls. (To assure that this is never forgotten, the church originally and since has built into its ordained ministry the office of deacon, understood as a key steward of *diakonia*.)[9]

A *critical* reading of the texts at hand uncovers the self-definition of the early community as expecting an imminent closure of history and thus a call to prepare for it by ordering its own life together as an immediate anticipation of behavior integral to the kingdom to be. Further, it saw itself commissioned to juxtapose this vision to the social, economic, and political circumstances around it, hence its rehumanizing care for those dehumanized by its society — widows, orphans, women, slaves, infants exposed, the sick, the poor, the old, and the dying. Critically understood also, the tiny Christian communities were outsiders to the structures of power and had no chance to undertake institutional strategies for social change even if their eschatological imminentism allowed for it. Again, a critical reading also defines the radical sharing as communitarian, not "communist," practice, as sometimes is carelessly alleged, for there was no collectivization of the means of production. Critical scholarship, therefore, poses the question as to how an eschatological anticipation in tension with the cultural givens and its associated communitarian practice can be carried over from what these texts meant to what they mean for us in places where eschatological schedules have been revised, communitarian visions confined to orders or utopian communities, but where some social power has

8. So the writer's *Word in Deed* (Grand Rapids: Eerdmans, 1975).

9. On the role of the diaconate, see *The COCU Consensus*, in *Churches in Covenant Communion and The COCU Consensus*, combined edition (Princeton: Consultation on Church Union, rev. ed. 1995), pp. 52-55.

been gained by the church, and the tension between the is and the ought to be and will be remains.

A *canonical* reading will locate these texts within the whole of Christian Scripture as read through its christological lens. Given the challenge of exact replication of early church practice, the hermeneutical principle of "analogy of faith" enters, clearer passages illumining difficult ones. When viewed in that light, the sharing of goods and healing of bodies are seen to be part of the larger biblical compassion for the hurt and the helpless. For example, there are far more biblical passages that urge care for the poor and the hungry than those mandating evangelism.[10] Thus, while not excluding a place for the literal practice of communitarian sharing and miraculous healing, these passages are exemplifications of a larger biblical mandate to serve the hurt and the helpless.

A christological-cum-canonical reading places the sharing and healing in the framework of Christ's teaching and practice. Here the aforementioned Samaritan story and its eschatological sequel are crucial:

> Then the king will say to those at his right hand, "Come, you that are blessed by my Father, inherit the kingdom prepared for you from the foundation of the world; for I was hungry and you gave me food, I was thirsty and you gave me something to drink, I was a stranger and you welcomed me, I was naked and you gave me clothing, I was sick and you took care of me, I was in prison and you visited me. . . . Truly I tell you, just as you did it to one of the least of these who are members of my family, you did it to me." (Matt. 25:34-36, 40)

Thus the clear christological warrant for outreach to the hungry, thirsty, homeless, poor, prisoner . . . And again, the same note struck:

> The Spirit of the Lord is upon me, because he has anointed me to bring good news to the poor. He has sent me to proclaim release to the captives and recovery of sight to the blind, to let the oppressed go free, to proclaim the year of the Lord's favor. (Luke 4:18)

The acts of *diakonia* are integral to the mission of Christ.

A canonical refrain is the reflection of the physicality entailed in the combination of these passages: Jesus Christ cares about bodies. How else

---

10. Ronald J. Sider, *Rich Christians in an Age of Hunger* (Nashville: Word Publishers, 1997).

for One who was the Word embodied? What else for One who called for the Samaritan care of the wounded on Jericho roads? How else for One bodily risen from the dead? For One who is with us now in his Body on earth? For One who in his glorified humanity rules in heaven? And for that Finale when there will be for us as well "the resurrection of the body"? So Archbishop Temple's observation that "Christianity is a materialist religion." Whatever the means, natural or supernatural, the church is called by its Lord to the care for bodies and is given the power of the Holy Spirit to be an instrument of *shalom* in things physical as well as spiritual.

The *contextual* sense of these passages requires our application of them to circumstances in our own time and place. How can we do with, to, and for our brothers and sisters in Christ what the first Christians did in their setting? When the church today is spread across the globe, and the boundaries of the community's bodies include, but go well beyond, the Christian poor and bereft in our town and our land? How can the Acts mandate not include the starving in the Sudan, and the raped and ravaged in Darfur and Rwanda? And, of course, the healings outside the temple gate in century one have their counterpart in the care for, and cure of, the sick of *any faith* or *no faith* outside the church doors in the church's history of medical ministries across the world. Unlike Peter and John who had no silver and gold, where we do have such wherewithal we are called to use it for the same ends of healing, not without the prayers and the like possibility of power over and above what the resources of modern medicine can bring to the task.

And when the End expected in apostolic times did not arrive on the expected schedule, what did the church do to carry out the diaconal ministry? The contextual sense takes us to the ways the wisdom of the Body of Christ by the power of the Holy Spirit sought to manifest this attribute of the church. We explore now the learnings from ecclesial history on what constitutes bodily servanthood in post-apostolic times.

Double *Diakonia*

It is said that Augustine, observing a food line outside a church, was heard to say, "We are feeding the hungry, but must ask, '*why* are they hungry and *what* is to be done about that?'" Hence the struggle of the church to minister to the need at hand, but also to go to the causes of the need. Thus developed the two forms of *diakonia,* described often as "social service" and "social action."

In a guide for pastors to help congregations understand the twofold character of *diakonia,* a story is told of a village at the foot of a mountain afflicted with the recurring crisis of accidents on the roadway that winds its way down the adjacent mountain. From time to time, drivers traveling at high speeds have failed to see a dangerous curve and hurtled over the side. The initial response of the townsfolk to these tragedies was to build a hospital to care for the injured. However, as the accidents continued, the town concluded that it was also necessary to construct a sturdy guardrail at the dangerous point to prevent the catastrophic fall. The parable points to the importance of ministration both after and before the fact. Thus the Good Samaritan story retold in terms of this dual responsibility entails both the binding up of wounds inflicted by the banditry and policing the Jericho road to prevent victimizing acts.

We need to interpret "double *diakonia*" in a communicable way in pastoral ministry. If *diakonia* is understood as servanthood to human need — ecclesially the "servant church" of Dulles's models — then the two forms it takes are *victim-care* and *victim-cause.* The first is the hospital ministry of the church, the compassionate outreach to the victims already lying on the Jericho roads; the second is the prevention of the hurt at its source.

Historically, there has been a progression from one to the other. Ecclesial efforts to bind up wounds — to feed the hungry, relieve the poor, care for the victims of war, oppression, injustice — have prompted Augustine's question and led to attacks on the causes of hunger, poverty, oppression, war, and injustice. That reach in back of the visible victim to the causes of victimhood has taken the church into the political, economic, and social arenas, and thus into political, economic, and social action. This step into addressing systemic issues — "victim-cause" servanthood — has brought with it some of the most heated controversies in recent church history and considerable soul-searching for guidance on whether and how institutionally oriented *diakonia* is a legitimate ecclesial undertaking. Here we draw on some learnings from the historic struggle with how best to address the issues of systemic *diakonia.*

Forms of Systemic Servanthood

Emerging in the history of church response to the Augustinian question has been a variety of approaches. They can be characterized as para-institutional, intra-institutional, and counter-institutional.

Para-institutional encounter with systemic victimhood assumes that unjust social, economic, and political structures are to be addressed by the church by establishing on their margins a visionary ecclesial community. The most faithful and fruitful address to the manifest evils of society is to demonstrate in the inner life of the church itself an alternative to the way of the world. As the church is a company of "resident aliens," it can best witness to the fallen world outside its walls what the divine intention is for that world. Thus the church in its very being is an eschatological sign of the kingdom challenging the social, economic, and political givens. The extent to which this witness is effective in altering the ways of the world is in the hands of a provident God. The goal is to be faithful, not to measure consequences by the standard of the successful.[11]

A second historic form of ministry to the hurt by addressing the systemic sources of abuse — intra-institutional — focuses on the "ministry of the laity." In the Body of Christ, only one percent is seen as needed for the stewardship of the mysteries in the church and 99 percent for the stewardship of the movements of the Body in the world. As noted earlier, one office is custodian of the identity of the Body, the other office of the vitality of the Body, although there is inextricability and even interchange. But here we take special note, vis-à-vis *diakonia*, that the laity are already located within the political, economic, and social structures, and as such, are

---

11. While the left-wing Reformation churches have been the historic custodians of this witness, today the writings of Stanley Hauerwas, striking the same note — hence his collegiality with Mennonite John Yoder — have had a wider impact. In days of pervasive cultural accommodation by the churches, the appeal of sharp juxtaposition of church and society is a powerful and also a needed Word to the churches. The increasing marginality of mainline churches in their host societies converges with the resident alien theology, becoming an inviting social ecclesiology. To the extent the latter is true, it must be asked whether the self-definition of the church as a company of resident aliens and the consequent withdrawal from direct institutional encounter is not an ideology in the sense of a set of ideas that justifies the status quo. The further question is whether this approach, standing alone, is not a reductionist view of the church's diaconal mandate. For all that, it is a historic option in cultural encounter, and should not be excluded from the diversity of stances for a church discerning the signs of its times.

positioned for an apostolate preeminently in that arena. They are the "church scattered," which has moved out from the "church gathered" to servanthood in structures of society.

What does that ministry entail? The same threefold office of Christ that the ministry of identity continues, but in the idiom and setting of the world in which they exercise their primary vocation. The workplace is the paradigmatic location for the exercise of that ministry, although the worlds of leisure, retirement, and family, etc. constitute their own places of ministry of the whole people of God. Laity live out their intra-institutional ministry when they speak the prophetic word in their workplace or other setting in witness to *shalom;* when they "priest" the sufferer in that setting; when they strive to conform that place to the norms of the royal rule of Jesus Christ.[12] The rich ecumenical research for the last half-century on the hows, whens, and wheres of *diakonia* within the structures of society is available for the pastor who is called to "equip the saints for their ministry" in those locales.[13]

The most familiar form of systemic servanthood is its counter-institutional expression, that associated with the language of "social action." In this mode the church, as church, engages the political, social, and economic powers. In contemporary form, such encounter may involve participation in the political process, or in social protest, or in economic boycott in support of causes and measures that reflect norms of justice, peace, and order, or the "middle axioms" that develop as "the mind of the church" in a given time and place and scale down the more general standards to guidelines applicable to particular circumstances.[14]

---

12. See George Peck and John S. Hoffman, eds., *The Laity in Ministry* (Valley Forge, Pa.: Judson Press, 1984), pp. 109-25 and *passim.*

13. The former Center for the Ministry of the Laity at Andover Newton, under the leadership of Richard Broholm, has pioneered this relating of the threefold office to the ministry of the laity in secular institutions, a project taken up since by the *Center for Seeing Things Whole*, under the leadership of David Specht, www.seeingthingswhole.org.

14. "Middle axioms" or "middle principles" that sought to scale down general axioms and principles "halfway" to particular issues (justice for black citizens in housing, jobs, public accommodations, and education, for example), an important development in ecumenical ethics in an earlier period (John Bennett, Ronald Preston, et al.), lost momentum for a while to too-quick affiliation of faith and the specifics of party or position on a particular issue or the return to abstraction in ethics, but are making a comeback in matters ecclesial and social ethical as the alternatives prove destructive or irrelevant.

Pastoral Decisions

The pastor is faced with the question of how to participate in and support the ecclesial graces of *diakonia*. To the obvious charge of preaching and teaching the biblical message of *diakonia,* making the congregation aware as well of the ecclesial middle axioms on particular issues, challenging any simple fusion of gospel and person, party or policy, as did the Barmen Declaration, and risking application of axioms general and middle in personal action, there remains the issue of the role of the congregation in diaconal witness and its relation to other ecclesial venues for the same.

As noted, the church early faced this question of the structure of diaconal ministry by developing the office of deacon and its derivative diaconate. While it has taken different turns in the history of the church, its original and continuing role is to be an instrument of the congregation in ministering to human need in the congregation and sometimes in victim-care outside the church doors as well.[15] The pastor can interpret to the congregation this historic role in reinforcing the congregation's commitment to *diakonia* of this kind.

More challenging is the move within the congregation to victim-cause ministry, when partisanships — political, economic, and social — begin to manifest themselves. This is reason for every congregation having a designated sub-community within the congregation for the nurture of this charism. Often it is called a "mission" committee, as the systemic issues are by definition in the realm of outreach. However, such can also be the catalyst for victim-care ministries. For example, through its mission committee a congregation may decide to address the crisis of homelessness in its community and choose to host for several days each month a group of the community's homeless citizens. In doing so, it may decide to participate in a candlelight vigil in the community to highlight the problem and press for legislation that funds housing for the homeless or jobs or mental health services that will enable the homeless to make their way out of their plight, moving the congregation through its representatives from victim-care to victim-cause.

The congregation may also determine to focus on one or more social issues with specific structures to so steward. Thus a committee responsible for a food bank in the congregation or for the homeless project itself may

15. *BEM,* p. 27.

be put in place, with Augustine's question always being asked and fitting actions taken.

To implement or even to launch these congregational ventures, other ecclesial structures may be entailed or required. Thus "extra-parochial" or "para-church" movements and institutions have emerged in the history of both victim-care and victim-cause.

Extra-parochial venues are those that work in conjunction with congregations. These para-groups may be in the community itself or beyond its borders, often well beyond them. At the community level, councils of churches provide a setting in which people from a variety of different congregations can join together to achieve social goals. Extra-parochial organizations beyond the community level include organizations such as Habitat for Humanity which builds homes for the dispossessed, Church World Service, and World Vision, all of them notable for their effectiveness, especially so in victim-care.

Pastors and congregations can address diaconal challenges beyond their borders through their own state, regional, and national denominational forms. The civil rights movement again provides a clear exemplification. Clergy and laity in mainline churches were brought into voter registration campaigns, demonstrations, and acts of civil disobedience through denominational social action agencies.[16] At the same time, and often with leadership from denominations now joined together, the National Council of Churches recruited 40,000 of the 200,000 church members at the historic March on Washington. In that same march, African American congregations and denominations accounted for many more, and were the front line of recruitment for civil rights actions in communities and states across the nation. Roman Catholic bodies weighed in similarly on this and other issues, and its National Council of Catholic Bishops has had a strong voice on multiple social issues over the decades.

When witness for a social cause becomes too closely associated with particular secular policies, programs, or persons, the gospel is compromised and needs the Barmen corrective. Indeed, history catches up with such confusions and the church pays a heavy price.

In some traditions, the Reformed for example, the words of Paul — "But when we are judged by the Lord, we are disciplined so that we may not be condemned along with the world" (Acts 11:32) — are interpreted in

16. For summaries, see *Social Action* 36, no. 4 (December 1969).

terms of a third Reformation mark of the church, along with Word and Sacrament: church discipline. A failure in conduct is warrant for exclusion from church membership, and where there is no church discipline, there is a question of whether the church there exists.

Twentieth-century examples of exclusion based on such discipline are found where racism is seen as theological in nature — the worship of another god — warranting the exclusion of a church body from a larger Reformed fellowship. The ousting of a South African church body from the World Alliance of Reformed Churches for its espousal of apartheid teaching and practice is a case in point. The Reformed tradition underscores the importance of sanctification in believers, so the stress on church discipline comes naturally as a mark of a faithful church.

Is the insistence that *diakonia* is integral to the church's very existence a following through ecclesially of James's declaration that "faith apart from works is barren" (James 2:20)? Indeed James thought in ecclesial terms in his letter, concerned as he was about the church's behavior toward the poor:

> If a poor person in dirty clothes comes in, and if you take notice of the one wearing fine clothes and say, "Have a seat here, please," while to the one who is poor you say, "Stand there," or, "Sit at my feet," have you not made distinctions among yourselves, and become judges with evil thoughts? (James 2:2-4)

His many injunctions to "be doers of the word, and not merely hearers" (James 1:22) are in an ecclesial context, encouraging "generous acts of giving," warning rich people of their temptations to live the oppressor's life of luxury, and counseling the ways of mercy and justice.

Luther, with his emphasis on salvation by faith alone, judged this letter an "epistle of straw" for its perceived rejection of Pauline teaching. However, it was Luther who also insisted that true faith is "busy in love," and had to deal with the antinomians who thought his gospel carried with it no law as the grateful obedience that flowed from genuine faith.[17]

While James insisted on the importance of ecclesial *diakonia*, he did not say that where there was failure in it, therefore, no church existed. Nor did Paul or Peter with their sharp strictures against the absence of *diakonia*.

17. See the writer's entry "Antinomianism," in *Dictionary of Christian Theology* (Philadelphia: Westminster Press, 1983), p. 27.

Those who demanded discipline as necessary for the faithfulness of the church to the point of exclusion made their case on kerygmatic grounds — racism as a failed Word — not on conduct alone. Further, the Reformed tradition, while considering its emphasis on sanctification and its deployment of discipline, did not deny the status of church to those who differed. This was a "church dividing" issue, not a church-denying one. And now that same tradition has moved to the point of mutual admonitions and the sharing of charisms with Lutherans on this disputed question.

There is a way to honor the importance of *diakonia* as a sign of the Spirit in a faithful church, but recognize a distinction from the role of *kerygma* and *leitourgia* in understanding the nature of the church. The imagery of Peter and Paul is a clue. Following the Pauline metaphor of the church as the Body, each speaks of sickness and death in connection with the absence of *diakonia*. Where the church gives little or no evidence of servanthood within or without, it is a sick Body. While alive, its condition may even be "sick unto death." The failure of *diakonia* puts the church under judgment. While still the church, if bearing the foundational marks of *kerygma* and *leitourgia,* it is in peril and will receive the punishment attendant thereto. "Woe to you" is a prophetic word to the church similar to that of the prophet calling the people of Israel to account. Still chosen, still alive by the grace of God alone, this people will receive the chastising due a disobedient people. To whom much is given much will be expected, and the failures will show up in consequences that follow disobedience.

Thus the difference in role between the first two signs of the Spirit — *kerygma* and *leitourgia* — and *diakonia* has to do with their respective roles. The first are the fontal marks of the church. Without them no church, and no channels of the grace that makes for a full and healthy Body of Christ. The latter signs of the Spirit — *diakonia* now, and *koinonia* to be treated subsequently — are consequential gifts of the Spirit. Returning to the Pauline imagery, their presence or absence indicates the temperature in the Body of Christ, its sickness or health.

Yet it is also true that there is death as well as sickness in the New Testament accounts of disobedience in *diakonia*. But it is not the death of the body as such but death *in* the Body. It is members that die, the atrophy of parts of the Body. The death is to a limb, the withering of a Body part, some at the Table, the Ananiases and Sapphiras who eat and drink judgment to themselves, not discerning the Body and thus failing to receive its life-giving Spirit.

If *kerygma* and *leitourgia* are the fontal graces and *diakonia* a flowing one, then the justification of the church by Word and Sacrament issues in its sanctification. Thus we arrive at a way of describing the third attribute of the church: its *sanctity* ranged alongside its *apostolicity* and *catholicity.*

As "sanctification" is associated with holiness in the life of the believing subject, the sanctity of the church, in this comparable sense (there is another sense alluded to earlier to which we shall return), has to do with its subjective holiness. While holiness in both believer and church can be understood in a wide-ranging sense that includes piety and religious practice,[18] here, as earlier noted, it is associated with deeds of care, the good works of *diakonia.*

As good works do not make a good person, but a good person — one saved by grace through faith — does good works (Luther), so the good works of the church do not make it the church. But a good church — saved by grace through faith — does good works. Therein lies the difference between the first two signs and attributes and the one under consideration, and why the Reformation speaks about the church's existence as grounded in preached Word and celebrated Sacrament, *kerygma* and *leitourgia,* or as it is named in the creeds and we have interpreted these terms — as apostolicity and catholicity. Where these are present, fontal grace brings with it the flowing grace of the works of *diakonia.* Where these are not visible the church is in peril, and under judgment; the Body is sick and may be sick unto death. Yet, as with the justified Christian, so with the justified church, it may exist even when this sign is seen only by God. Is this then "the church invisible"?

The Church Invisible

Some traditions find a place for this teaching while others attack it vigorously. What are the issues?

A rigorous version of the Reformed tradition shaped by its conception of election assumes the reality of a church invisible. Its theory of double predestination stipulates that only God knows the elect. While participa-

18. So treated in Dorothy and Gabriel Fackre, *Christian Basics: A Primer for Pilgrims* (Grand Rapids: Eerdmans, 6th printing, 2000), pp. 101-11.

tion in the visible community of elect is in accord with the purposes of God, the divine sovereignty is not guaranteed by these visibilities. Others with less stringent norms may take the same tack by simply saying that "It is God who sees the heart," making the practice of church membership no doorway to eternal salvation.

The purposes of God may be further removed from the church visible by versions of both of the foregoing. A strict predestinarianism has allowed for the election of the "righteous pagan" by the "uncovenanted mercies of God." The second view, that only God sees the heart, may be stretched to include all those in any and every religion, or no religion, who as "good people" are acceptable to God, a view that may have little interest in personal eschatological outcomes, and one sometimes formulated ecclesiologically as membership in the "hidden church."

The foregoing presupposes God's freedom to constitute "church" over and above or beyond the usual means of grace in Word and Sacrament. Here, however, we have moved the discussion of invisibility to another attribute. In so doing, we remind the sharpest critics of the concept of an invisible church that they too assume such concerning this attribute. No one who is deeply concerned about the dangers of works-righteousness wants to defend an ecclesiology which holds that the church rises and falls with the church's good works. As the believer is at the same time justified and a sinner, so the church is at the same time justified and sinful, in both cases justified in spite of the absence of good works and thus by faith alone — in the believer's case the grace offered in Word and Sacrament and received in faith, and in the church's case through the administration of Word and Sacrament received in faith. Thus though the attribute is invisible to the eye of sight, the church is real by the work of the Holy Spirit invisibly, or as indicated in Chapter 3, discernible by the eye of faith.

This latter view is often stated this way: the church is holy, not because of our holiness but because the holy God is present. As the believer shares in an "alien righteousness," so too does the church. In the former, by the receipt of saving grace; in the latter, by being its home and means. The "sanctity" of the church resides in its being the household of the holy God whose presence and power are available, not because of who we in the church are, but because of who the Christ of unconditional love in his Body is. Thus the objectivity of sanctity counts against the missing subjectivity. Grace is offered even in a community of sinners, and, as in the

Donatist controversy, is accessible even when its ministerial custodians are lacking in the desired conduct.[19]

With this said, we nevertheless face the same dispute earlier mentioned. In the Christian life, is not true faith fruitful in works, and therefore where there is faith it is busy in love? Transposed ecclesially, how can there be a true church of faith through Word and sacrament that does not also show itself in diaconal works of love?

In both cases, cautions are in order for those ready to declare the workless believer dead in sin, or the church dead in its absence of deeds. Caution 1: Do we bring our own criterion to bear on what constitutes deeds of love? Is this coterminous with the divine norm? Caution 2: Can our own sinful and finite instruments of discernment always detect what is the case in the believer or in the church? Our vision is not the equivalent of the eye of God. Caution 3: If the foundational grace-faith in the Christian life is present in a believer or the fontal Word and Sacrament in the church, will it not ultimately produce the fruits promised in these seeds? God's timetable is not the same as ours. Caution 4: Where there is a workless believer and a loveless church, we can be sure that judgment will follow in both time and eternity, so evidenced by the fate of Ananias and Sapphira, and members in like jeopardy in the Corinthian church. The holy God, present by the divine promise, will not tolerate unholiness in either case. Our merits do not establish our salvation, nor do those of the church establish its existence. Our demerits to do not disqualify our salvation when acknowledged in penitence and faith. The same is true of the church where its message in Word and Sacrament is set forth and received. Thus, finally, the church is holy by the grace of its objective though invisible attributes, which we are called to make manifest. Failing to do so, we live with the hot coals of the divine love that will take their toll even as its warmth will spur and empower us to do deeds in kind. The unmerited gift of sanctity before God calls us to "be what you are!" before the world. And the promise of Christ is that the church of Word and sacrament will not be denied discernible fruits of the Spirit. To trust that this is so propels us forward to be what we are.

19. Yet other versions of the church invisible have reference to the inviolable "communion of saints," those who have died in Christ and share now in the church triumphant. Even those who believe all the foregoing, but wrongly disconnect the purposes of God from the promises of God to be among us in the church visible, hold to this dimension of the church's invisibility.

Again, the New Testament images sum up an attribute of the church. The church is holy because it is the pentecostal *people* of the triune God. Its unalterable sanctity derives from its existence as a chapter in the Story of God. As human as well as divine, its people wander into unholy ways. Yet its sanctity, *coram Deo,* is not dissolved by their demerits, and what is seen by the eye of God will somewhere, somehow, also been seen by the human eye.

The church is holy because it is the *Body* of Christ on earth, an organism sanctified by his promise and presence. For all the human poisons in its bloodstream, it yet lives by a grace not its own, one that will manifest itself in times of health as well as sustaining it in its states of sickness.

The church is holy because the Holy Spirit brought this *Temple* to be. At Pentecost, the Spirit made a building that will last until the End. The moneychangers may erect their stalls and ply their trade, but the winds of the Spirit of the Son will do a cleansing work when so willed by the triune God. To the fore in this exploration of the diaconal sign of the Spirit has been the outreach, rather than the inreach, aspect of the church's nature. The needs of that wider world are so commanding today, and the church's capacity to serve is so ample in mainline Western Christianity, that such an emphasis is only fitting. But elsewhere — in the church of the global south? — both the requirement and capacity to respond to the needs of the brothers and sisters within may well be to the fore. Faithfulness to the New Testament standard means a signing that is both inreach and outreach, the church of a given time and place discerning as best it can its resources and mandates.

CHAPTER 7

Koinonia: *Life Together and Unity*

D ivision is everywhere. How can we speak of unity? Like sanctity, however, the promises of Christ are stronger than our performances. He
grants to the undeserving a unity reflecting the oneness the Son has with
the Father in the Spirit (John 17:21). By the power of the Holy Spirit, there
is an ecclesial *koinonia* that mirrors the divine Life Together, not because
of our weak efforts at unity, but in spite of our strong drives toward disunity. Therefore, there is an ontological unity we *already do have,* before
any we seek empirically.

In what does this unity consist? Again, like sanctity, the counter-
evidence is ample. But the unity "we have" is not without its indicators. The
Nairobi Assembly of the World Council of Churches was bold to declare:

> Despite all the divisions which have occurred in the course of the
> centuries, there is a real though imperfect communion which contin-
> ues to exist among those who believe in Christ and are baptized in his
> name.[1]

How can such a claim be made? The reason is that its participating
churches

---

1. "Message to the Churches," Nairobi Assembly, World Council of Churches, in David M. Paton, ed., *Breaking Barriers, Nairobi 1975* (Grand Rapids: Eerdmans, 1967), p. 272.

confess that Christ, true God and true Man, is Lord and that it is through him and in him alone that we are saved. Through the Spirit, they offer praises and thanksgiving to the Father who in his Son reconciles the world to himself. They proclaim the love of God, revealed by the Son who was sent by the Father, who brings new life to the human race, and who through the promise and gift of the Holy Spirit gathers together the people of the New Covenant as a communion of unity in faith, hope and love.[2]

A more recent study puts it in similar but terser terms:

> Visible Christian unity . . . exists already in virtue of our common faith which unites us in a single Savior. . . .[3]

It appears that the invisible unity of the church is inseparable from some very definite visibilities and audibilities. We examine them.

One of them is baptism.

> It reminds us that the gift of baptism makes us one with Christ our brother and it makes us sisters and brothers of each other.[4]

In the language of *BEM*:

> Through baptism, Christians are brought into union with each other and with the Church of every time and place. Our common baptism, which unites us to Christ, is thus a basic bond of unity.[5]

Baptism by water with the ecumenical formula, "In the name of the Father and of the Son and of the Holy Spirit," is a bonding with Christ and thus with the Body of Christ universal. Where such is practiced, the unity of the church begins to break forth, regardless of how estranged the institutional churches in fact are.

"Begins to break forth," yes, but the invisible/visible unity can only exist in its fullness through the union with the *totus Christus*. That bonding

2. "Message to the Churches," p. 272.

3. Carl Braaten and Robert Jenson, eds., *In One Body Through the Cross: The Princeton Proposal for Christian Unity* (Grand Rapids: Eerdmans, 2003), p. 13.

4. Donald Anderson, quoted in Edward A. Powers, *In Essentials, Unity: An Ecumenical Sampler* (New York: Friendship Press, 1982), p. 11.

5. *BEM*, p. 3.

with the total Christ has to do not only with birth of and into the Body of Christ but also nourishment of and by the Body of Christ. Again, *BEM:*

> The eucharistic communion with Christ, who nourishes the life of the Church, is at the same time communion with the body of Christ which is the Church. The sharing in one bread and the common cup in a given place demonstrates and effects the oneness of the sharers with Christ and with their fellow sharers in all times and places. It is in the eucharist that the community of God's people is fully manifested.[6]

The church is one in its common eating and drinking, however separated by institutional nomenclature.

> But let us not forget that "eucharist" always includes both word and sacrament . . . a proclamation and a celebration. . . .[7]

And what is this "proclamation"? According to Nairobi, it must include core christological and trinitarian teachings, the "common faith" of the church universal. It is no accident that the Faith and Order Commission of the World Council of Churches has produced a document attempting to identify just what that "common faith" is with its christological and trinitarian core, as in *Confessing the Apostolic Faith Today* with its exploration of the Nicene Creed. Thus, insofar as "the Word is preached" — one that witnesses to the triune God at work in the redemption of the world through Jesus Christ (the three creedal paragraphs), *koinonia* is present. Where the Story is told in preaching and teaching, there is the Word of the Father by the power of the Holy Spirit bringing the one church to be.

In these latter observations, we have looped back to the Reformation view of the marks of the church as "Word and Sacrament." These visibilities and audibilities are the means of grace through which the Holy Spirit keeps the Body of Christ alive. To the extent of their presence, the church is not only apostolic and catholic, but it is also one and holy. "One and holy" *coram Deo*, before God in its transcendent reality. But before the world? That is another matter.

---

6. *BEM*, p. 14.
7. *BEM*, p. 10.

It is no accident that *BEM* includes "ministry" in its threefold focus. The custodians of Word and Sacrament are those called by the church to be stewards of these mysteries. While ministry is much broader than the custodianship of Word and Sacrament — the ministry of the whole people of God, as earlier discussed — the guarding of the means of grace is crucial to the church's existence, its *esse.* The nature of that ministry is in dispute ecumenically, and continuing inquiry about the place of apostolic succession in ordained ministry is very important. But in the larger matter of the doctrine of the church, ecclesiology must include a custodial role for Word and Sacrament for the being of the one church.

The Gift and the Call

The unity before God signaled by Word and Sacrament calls for a unity before the world. What is *coram Deo* must also be *coram mundo*. Such is the mandate to "be what we are," to render empirically visible what is ontologically invisible. Under the title of "The Unity We Have and the Unity We Seek," the Princeton proposal asserts that

> Christians belong together . . . the unity that is already ours must appear more fully in our worship, our mission and the structures of our religious life.[8]

Ecumenism in its varied expressions is the quest to make manifest in our sight what is already the case in God's sight.

Since the beginnings of the church, this has been our burden. The church at Corinth is the showcase of the gift and claim. "Now you *are* the body of Christ, and individually members of it," declares Paul (1 Cor. 12:27). Before God the Body is healthy and whole, all the parts in place doing what they do, the church being what it is. Before the world, not so. The problem in Corinth is that:

> Each one of you says, "I belong to Paul," or "I belong to Apollos," or "I belong to Cephas," or "I belong to Christ." Has Christ been divided? (1 Cor. 1:12-13a)

---

8. Braaten and Jenson, eds., *In One Body,* p. 13.

This is analogous to parts of a human body, let's say a foot. Suppose it

> would say, "Because I am not a hand, I do not belong to the body," that would not make it any less part of the body. And if the ear would say, "Because I am not an eye, I do not belong to the body," that would not make it any less part of the body. If the whole body were an eye, where would the hearing be? If the whole body were hearing where would the sense of smell be? But as it is, God arranged the members in the body, each one of them, as he chose. If all were a single member, where would the body be? As it is, there are many members, yet one body. The eye cannot say to the hand, "I have no need of you," nor the head to the feet, "I have no need of you." . . . (1 Cor. 12:15-21)

This oft-quoted passage is not just an injunction to feuding factions and denominations to "get it together." It is an ontology of the church *coram Deo*. Just as the human body is a complex interacting unity of many members, so the church is *already* a unified organism. Thus at the close of his use of the human figure, Paul asserts, "Now you are the body of Christ and individually members of it" (1 Cor. 12:27). But what is true in God's sight, is not true in our sight. Hence the imperative that grows out of the indicative: be what you are!

Being what we are entails an honoring of "the other," a recognition that one cannot go it alone as church, but must respect, and integrate, the other charisms of Christ — parts of the body — into one's own being. Short of that mutuality, the Body is broken, distorted, maimed, disfigured, even absurd — "If the whole body were an eye, where would the hearing be?" The dissociated parts of the church empirical are called to mirror the wholeness of the Body ontological.

This challenge to the Body's empirical brokenness has been taken up in recent ecumenics by the call to complementarity. Cardinal Walter Kasper, Rome's ecumenical officer, has made a startling admission that even in the church that historically regards itself as the true Body of Christ, others being deficient,[9] there is recognition of the wounding of the Body:

---

9. So the judgment that some are churches through apostolic succession (viz., the Orthodox churches) though short of the fullness because not yet being in communion with Rome, and others, as is the case with Reformation churches, "ecclesial communities."

The Catholic Church too is wounded by the divisions of Christianity. Her wounds include the impossibility of concretely realizing fully her own Catholicity in the situation of division. Several aspects of being Church are better realized in other churches. So we can learn from each other in order to grow in the one truth of Jesus Christ, to comprehend and to realize more and more the richness he revealed to us. Thus since the Councils we Catholics learned a lot from our Protestant brothers and sisters about the importance of the word of God and its proclamation, and who knows only a little on orthodox icons gets aware what spiritual richness we can draw from them. The *oikoumenē* is a spiritual process, in which the question is not about a way backwards but about a way forwards by mutual exchange. . . . Ecumenism is no one-way street, but a reciprocal learning process — as stated in the ecumenical Encyclical *Ut unum sint* — an exchange of gifts.[10]

The acknowledgment of the importance of charisms brought by others to the Church of Rome is a significant ecumenical breakthrough.

In the framework of the ecclesiology set forth in this volume, the "wounding" goes deep. That is, it affects all the other signs of the Spirit and attributes of the church, and thus illustrates their close interrelationship. For one, where the church is divided, apostolicity is diminished. The fullness of the gospel *kerygma* proclaimed depends on the wholeness of the church, both in time and space. The eye of one tradition cannot say to the hand of another, "I have no need of you." The feet of an activist present church cannot say to the wisdom of the head of the church ancient, "I have no need of you." So too, the catholicity of the church, as here understood, requires the unity of the Body. No better illustration of that can be currently found than the ecumenical convergence document — BEM, to which attention has here been given, and for that reason. The charisms of the various traditions are brought together in the understanding of the central acts of *leitourgia,* and the ministries associated therewith, both clergy and lay. Equally true is the fullness of insight concerning, and the effective exercise of, *diakonia.* A church *together* brings resources and per-

---

10. Cardinal Walter Kasper, "Present Day Problems in Ecumenical Theology" in *Reflections, Volume 6: The 2003 Public Lectures* (Princeton: Center of Theological Inquiry, 2003), pp. 56-88, cited by Reinhard Hütter in *Bound to Be Free: Evangelical Catholic Engagements in Ecclesiology, Ethics, and Ecumenism* (Grand Rapids: Eerdmans, 2004), pp. 40-41. We shall take up Hütter's own point of view subsequent to that appearing in this important book.

spectives that are needed to address the crises that afflict the twenty-first century "flat earth" (Thomas Friedman), itself bound together by technological advances that bring with them commensurate perils and thus the need for unities in approach to solutions as never before.

The importance of unity is based not only on the ontological nature of the church as one, belonging to the Christ who is not divided, but because of who we are in our finitude and our fallenness. As creatures of a given time, space, and condition, and sinners with our own agendas, we need others to see things for what they are, not what we choose to, or are constricted by location to, make them out to be. Anthropology as well as ecclesiology and Christology themselves argue for unity, even as they themselves as doctrines are linked as reflection on interrelated chapters in the Story.

The need for "mutual exchange" and the overcoming of impoverishment in charisms in any one empirical church by learning from others was given significant expression in the recent Lutheran-Reformed dialogue in North America. From that exchange came the phrase "mutual affirmation and mutual admonition":

> In discovering our agreement on essential matters of the gospel, we have also recognized the important theological differences that remain between our churches. In such questions as the understanding of the Lord's Supper and Christology, these theological differences are, we believe, crucial for the ongoing ecumenical relations between these traditions. We view them not as disagreements that need to be overcome but as diverse witnesses to the one gospel that we confess in common. Rather than being church-dividing, the varying theological emphases among, and even within, these communities provide complementary expressions of the church's faith in the triune God. Throughout this document we employ the principle of "mutual affirmation and mutual admonition" to make the different theological emphases of these traditions fruitful for each other and for their common witness to the wider church. The theological diversity within our common confession provides both the complementarity needed for a full and adequate witness to the gospel (mutual affirmation) and the corrective reminder that every theological approach is a partial and incomplete witness to the gospel (mutual admonition).[11]

11. Keith F. Nickle and Timothy F. Lull, eds., *A Common Calling: The Witness of Our Reformation Churches in North America Today* (Minneapolis: Augsburg Fortress, 1993), p. 66.

An example of this mutual corrigibility appears in the interpretation of the eucharist. Thus,

> For our present task this means that all the divergent assertions and rejections among Lutherans and Reformed have a right to be heard and affirmed. But these interpretations are not uncritically received and definitive. Seen in the light of the beginnings, they are inclusive of each other, not exclusive, each of them necessary to express the fullness of the biblical witness and its patristic appropriation. At the same time they warn and admonish both sides not to overlook the shortcoming and dangers in pressing for one side's concerns only. . . . Lutheran Christians need to understand and uphold the Reformed emphasis on the Spirit, the trinitarian work of God, and the assembly of the faithful. Reformed Christians need to understand and uphold the Lutheran insistence on the incarnational paradox, the real Christ in bread and wine, and the objectivity of God's gift in Word and sacrament. Both sides must heed the concerns of the partners, if not as a guide to their own formulations, then at least as no trespassing signs for the common forms of the churches' witness to the reality of God's action in the Supper. . . .[12]

Here is a recognition that the fullness of the meaning of the Supper in the Body-before-God entails the accents of both traditions, a complementarity that must be embodied in moves toward the unity of the church on earth, in this case the modest advance of "full communion," but a formula that points beyond to larger unities yet to be achieved.

An example of a dramatic step toward that larger unity that works with the premise of both Cardinal Kasper and the Lutheran-Reformed agreement is the recent Lutheran-Catholic *Joint Declaration on the Doctrine of Justification.* It is expressed in the give-and-take on aspects of that doctrine, as for example, "Justification as Forgiveness of Sins and Making Righteous":

> When Lutherans emphasize that the righteousness of Christ is our righteousness, their intention is above all to insist that the sinner is granted righteousness before God in Christ through the declaration of forgiveness, and that only in union with Christ is one's life re-

---

12. Nickle and Lull, eds., *A Common Calling,* pp. 48-49.

newed. When they stress that God's grace is forgiving love ("the favor of God"), they do not thereby deny the renewal of the Christian's life. They intend rather to express that justification remains free from human cooperation and is not dependent on the life-giving effects of grace in human beings. When Catholics emphasize the renewal of the interior person through the reception of grace imparted as a gift to the believer, they wish to insist that God's forgiving grace always brings with it a gift of new life which in the Holy Spirit becomes effective in active love. They do not thereby deny that God's gift of grace in justification remains independent of human cooperation.[13]

Embedded in this declaration are the premises of mutuality and complementarity. Each tradition has its historic emphasis, protective of a critical dimension of justification — the Lutheran accent on grace as pardon toward the believer, the Catholic accent on grace as power in the believer. Each acknowledges the stewardship of the other and explicitly declares that its own emphasis does not preclude that of the other. While the language of mutual affirmation and admonition or Cardinal Kasper's generous recognition of the need for mutual learning is not explicit, it is certainly implicit in this critical new advance on a historic church-dividing doctrine.

The foregoing has to do with wider matters of ecumenism. However, "where the rubber hits the road" for the working pastor is at other levels: the denomination of which one is a part and the congregation one serves. How is the unity of the church and the gift and demand of *koinonia* to be there understood? Indeed, in a pastoral systematics, this question is front and center.

The doctrinal affirmations and empirical observations regarding this sign of the Spirit and attribute of the church obtain in the church ecumenical, the church denominations, and the church local. Thus where the apostolicity and catholicity of Word and Sacrament — marks of the church, and thus special signs and attributes — are present, there also is the People of God, the Body of Christ, and the Temple of the Spirit. The import of such a declaration for the subject at hand is that the gift of *koinonia* is given ontologically to that denomination and congregation,

---

13. The Lutheran World Federation and the Roman Catholic Church, *Joint Declaration on the Doctrine of Justification* (Grand Rapids: Eerdmans, 1999), pp. 18-19.

and as such, brings with it the promise and mandate of empirical manifestation. The church national and the church local that live under Word and Sacrament are in God's eyes already one and therefore can be and must be one in human eyes.

How fundamental and pressing this affirmation and its implications are in the present state of the church at the levels in question! In the early years of the twenty-first century the mainline churches in the West have been rent with controversy and the threat of schism. The partisanships of the culture-wars reappear in the contentious atmosphere of many denominations, as well as do serious theological differences embodied by one fractious camp after another. As in the United Church of Christ used in Chapter 2 as a laboratory of learning, Lutheran, Methodist, Presbyterian, Episcopalian, and other oldline denominations are "divided and dividing." What is the bearing of this sign of the Spirit in such a time?

To the extent that these national bodies are in their corporate texts and traditions stewards of the Word and sacraments, they bear the marks of the church. As such, they *already* are granted a unity *coram Deo*. With it comes the promise of the Spirit's work in their midst to actualize the *koinonia* they already enjoy before God. So promised, so mandated. As with the wider ecumenism, there is a "unity we seek" based on "the unity we have." How different would circumstances be if we would view the fissiparous plight of the mainline churches in the light of this gift given, promise made, and command issued? It would reverse the conventional wisdom of another day that "doctrine divides but practice unites." To share in a doctrine of the church that affirms the gift of a transcendent unity with its derivative possibilities in time and space by the work of the Holy Spirit would be to re-energize the quest for a life together within our denominational church home. One small piece of evidence that this is so comes from the earlier cited 2005 action of the General Synod of the United Church of Christ that has been a window into mainline problems and possibilities. Its reassertion in a resolution of Jesus Christ as Lord and Savior, divine and human in nature as stated and presupposed in its rites and official teaching, and thus a church grounded in Word and Sacrament was a moment when the feuding parties came together for a "mutual affirmation" that can lay the groundwork for living with a diversity of "mutual admonition."

The same doctrinal premises apply to life in a congregation. Where the marks of the church are present, its apostolicity and catholicity thus manifest, it has, before God, both a sanctity and unity and the promise, mandate, and possibility of such in its common life. We are back where these ruminations in ecclesiology began in *Under the Steeple*, but with the premises now clarified and the warrants for a life together grounded in the divine-human ontology of the church and related to its signs, marks, and attributes. Where the Word is faithfully preached and the sacraments rightly celebrated in a given congregation, that people of God is the Body of Christ and a Temple where the Holy Spirit calls its inhabitants to be what it is, to actualize the unity already granted. Imagine the difference it would make in a conflicted St. John's-by-the-Gas-Station if it well understood the grace there given that could make for these mutualities.

What about the visible state of *koinonia* in St. John's-by-the-Gas-Station? Tony Campolo, seeking to answer the question "Can mainline denominations make a comeback?" in his recent book by the same name, answers his question by urging, "Let's try to offer something that people . . . desperately crave — *community.*"[14] The old church by the gas station needs to learn from the new megachurch near the mall. Thousands do attend these new institutions, but their secret is the small group:

> Those who are into pastoral ministry often contend that it is in small groups that church happens. The Holy Spirit is most likely to come, they say, when people in small groups meet in total openness to one another. . . . That special kind of fellowship that the Bible calls *koinonia.* . . . Such small-group experiences are an antidote to a social sickness that leaves so many of us estranged and anonymous.[15]

For this writer, who began pastoral ministry attempting to "discern the signs of the times" and, with many others, put *koinonia* to the fore as response to a depersonalized society, this of course has a familiar ring. However, at that time the place of *koinonia* was the congregation itself. Now in the era of megachurches, it is in small groups within the congregation that true "life together" is said to take place.[16]

14. Tony Campolo, *Can Mainline Denominations Make a Comeback?* (Valley Forge, Pa.: Judson Press, 1995), p. 44.

15. Campolo, *Can Mainline Denominations Make a Comeback?* pp. 44, 45. For the "première" website on the subject of small groups in the church, see the one significantly titled "Lifetogethertoday."

16. In the 1950s too, attention was given to the small group, as in the popular book by John Casteel, *Spiritual Renewal Through Personal Groups* (New York: Association Press, 1957).

As *koinonia* is one of the signs of the Spirit and attributes of the church, there is no question that its visible recovery, either *within* the congregation, or *as* the congregation, is, at the local church level as well as in a wider ecumenism, both a manifestation and mandate of the Holy Spirit. Let there be an admonition given to the mainline churches from their evangelical brothers and sisters where New Testament life together is lacking. And let their own gift of *koinonia* be shared with oldline congregations.

However, if we can learn some lessons from the pilgrimage of mainline Protestantism through the decades tracked earlier, it is: be wary of the reduction of the nature and mission of the church to one of its signs. Be wary as well of conceiving the church essentially in terms of its response to the questions of the era in which it finds itself. Its "essence" is richer, and it must pose the question not asked by a given time and place. Interestingly, the cycle through which the mainline churches lived in the twentieth century could well be repeated by thriving evangelical constituencies. In this case it is learning, for example, that *koinonia* without also a visible *diakonia* is an impoverishment of the church's being. The move of the Saddleback congregation and its pastor, Rick Warren, to shift its eye and thus also its hand outward to the plight of the nation of Rwanda, is not unlike the move outward of the mainline churches from the *koinonia* of the 1950s to the *diakonia* of the 1960s.[17] And there is, in the light of the latter's twentieth-century learnings, and most important the New Testament account of the first Christians and the classical attributes of the church universal, the need for solid Christian doctrine and an authentic sacramental and liturgical life to keep company with the healing intimacies of the small group and the outreach to the victims on the Jericho road.

The pursuit of empirical unity and genuine life together is no optional venture. Consequences follow, dire by Corinthian record. In the same letter, indeed, just before the Pauline commentary on the body (chapter 12) is the judgment passed on those who come to the common Table, the intended unity of the church in microcosm:

---

17. See the cover story of *Christianity Today* 49, no. 10 (October 2005), "Purpose-Driven in Rwanda: Rick Warren Has a Sweeping Plan to Defeat Poverty." The enthusiasm and dynamism of the evangelical experience is reflected in these plans and descriptions. It can be hoped that the sobriety about human nature and the ambiguity of historical advance that is part of the theological wisdom of classical Christianity is a charism that the ecumenical church can share with its evangelical brothers and sisters without dampening the enthusiasm or weakening the dynamism.

Whoever, therefore, eats the bread or drinks the cup in an unworthy manner will be answerable for the body and blood of the Lord. Examine yourselves, and only then eat of the bread and drink of the cup. For all who eat and drink without discerning the body, eat and drink judgment against themselves. (1 Cor. 11:27-29)

Tough talk. Transposed to the issue of the unity of the church: those who perpetuate the disunity or fail to embody the charism of *koinonia,* pay dearly. The disconnect between the wholeness of the church — its life together before the divine Life Together — and the broken church on earth will take a toll on the latter. What we know of the Pauline complaint follows suit. Some members of the church were disrupting the communion meal by rushing forward and denying to others a place at the Table. Indeed, pursuing the analogy of Table and Body, Paul makes the connection that follows:

For this reason many of you are weak and ill, and some have died. (1 Cor. 11:30)

When disruption occurs at the Table, bodily suffering and even death ensues. Likewise, when disunity exists and *koinonia* is lacking in the Body of Christ, that organism also sickens and sometimes dies. Unity is medicine for the sick and dying body/Body.

As with *diakonia,* so with *koinonia,* where the church does not show either sign of the Spirit at a given time and place or in the splendor of their fullness, it does not cease to be the church, but it is a church under judgment. And that judgment means a sick church, even a sickness unto death.

In sum, where the Holy Spirit pours out the *kerygma,* the gospel being heralded and apostolicity so granted, and the same Spirit gifts us with *leitourgia* centered in the catholicity of the Bath and the Meal, there is the Body of Christ. Being a body as well as Body, human as well as divine, it is always broken by our sin and thus is, as with the believer, *simul iustus et peccator,* living only by these means of grace. Those visible means — Word and Sacrament — assure us, as well, of the invisible gifts of unity and sanctity, even in our brokenness, attributed to us not by our merit but by Christ's promises. Yet, when we show no gratitude for graces both visible and invisible, the Body/body moves from brokenness to disease and the threat of death. Where there are no visible signs of faithfulness in *koinonia* and *diakonia,* there the Spirit of the Son comes in judgment, as that same Spirit came to the Corinthian congregation. Without visible unity and visible sanctity the church graced by apostolicity and catholicity is in peril. Still the church, it is the church under judgment. If this is our lot today, God have mercy on us and grant us the grace to respond to our gifts in grateful obedience.

The Communion of Saints

What is the range of the church's *koinonia?* Surely as "catholic" in the geographic sense it runs across the world. But what of time as well as space? That too. The church universal stretches from Beginning to End. What of beyond time and space? "I believe in . . . the communion of saints." That *communio* bridges earth and heaven. There are

> two dimensions of the one church. It is important to acknowledge, as did the Reformers, that the saints on earth and the saints in heaven are linked together in a mystic communion that can never be shaken or terminated.[18]

In an extended discussion of the creedal affirmation, Donald Bloesch joins Luther, the Mercersburg theologians, P. T. Forsyth, William Temple, Robert Jenson, a company of hymn writers, and of course, the notable theologians of the Great Tradition in earlier centuries, in reflecting on what this life together of saints on earth and heaven entails. As we have traced the theological ups and downs of the mainline churches in the twentieth century by occasional attention to one of them, the United Church of Christ, it is fitting to be in dialogue at the close of this work with a theologian within its ranks. Donald Bloesch's views on this subject may be a surprise to evangelicals who count him as a premier spokesperson, as well as news to those of his own church.[19]

Interpreting selected texts of Scripture through the eyes of the Great

---

18. Donald G. Bloesch, *The Last Things: Resurrection, Judgment, Glory* (Downers Grove, Ill.: InterVarsity Press, 2004), p. 161.

19. Bloesch is the only theologian in our time to have written a seven-volume systematic theology, *Christian Foundations.* Well respected in the evangelical world, he is too-little read and engaged in the wider circles of church and academy.

Tradition and its hymns sung to and for "all the saints," the church on earth and in heaven "have fellowship and union with one another."[20] The church invisible that has gone before us is inextricably bound together with the church visible, the Church Triumphant linked to the Church Militant, and thus a "real interaction between the faithful in heaven and the faithful on earth."[21] For Bloesch this means "remembrance, mutual intercession and conversation . . . [albeit] sharply distinguished from 'spirit communication' or necromancy, which is clearly forbidden in Scripture. . . ."[22]

What does this mutuality mean? Bloesch argues that the saints pray along *with us* and also pray *for us*. And we too can pray *for them* in their journey in heaven.[23] Can we pray *to them*?

> What about the age-old practice of petition *to* the saints? . . . Because of the inveterate temptation to view the saints as mediators of redemption, we should generally refrain from invoking the saints in glory, but we may request their aid in our prayers to God and Christ. . . . As a Reformed churchman I am comfortable with the Anglican position that we should honor the saints without promoting or engaging in the practice of invocation.[24]

In spite of this caution and caveat, Bloesch cites "these perspicacious comments of Archbishop Temple":

> Do not be content to pray for them. Let us also ask them to pray for us. . . . Doubtless the ministry of love continues, but let us seek it, ask for it, claim it. . . .[25]

Donald Bloesch is to be commended for reminding both evangelicals and ecumenicals of a dimension of the church too seldom taken into account in either theology or practice. The Body of Christ on earth, which has also been the focus of this work, is inseparable from the Body of Christ in heaven. A full-orbed doctrine of the church will attend to the commu-

---

20. The Second Helvetic Confession, quoted by Bloesch, *Christian Foundations* (Downers Grove, Ill.: InterVarsity Press, 2006), p. 161.

21. Bloesch, *Christian Foundations*, p. 163.

22. Bloesch, *Christian Foundations*, p. 162.

23. Bloesch, *Christian Foundations*, p. 167.

24. Bloesch, *Christian Foundations*, p. 165.

25. Bloesch, *Christian Foundations*, p. 167.

nion of saints on earth with those in heaven. We recall that twofold reality in our hymnody as Bloesch points out — "O blest communion, fellowship divine, We feebly struggle, they in glory shine"[26] — eminently so in the eucharist and especially so on "worldwide communion Sunday" which is also "otherworldwide."

But it is more than recollection, the "remembrance" in Bloesch's trinity of relationships. The communion of the saints is also his second term, "mutual intercession." Let pastors pray for the dead as well as for the mourners! Of a Sunday in the pastoral prayer and encouraging the same in the prayer time of the people that is now part of so many services. Surely too at Christian burial, where in many standard liturgies there is a place for prayer for the deceased. Impetus for such can be as minimal as Luther's counsel to speak those words if so moved by a love for the departed. And more by an ecclesiology accompanying it that understands the bond between the church on earth and the church in heaven, and by an eschatology that makes room for a growth in grace even beyond the gates of death.[27] And why would not this mutuality also include assists from beyond? As in Zinzendorf's trust that

> The prayers of the saints in heaven directly benefit their brothers and sisters who are still on their earthly pilgrimage.[28]

What then about Bloesch's third linkage of ecclesial earth and heaven, "mutual . . . conversation"? A reference to an encounter reported by J. B. Phillips appears to be an example of this:

> . . . in a time of acute distress Phillips . . . was consoled by words of encouragement from C. S. Lewis, who had only then been translated into glory but who appeared visibly to Phillips on two occasions.[29]

What do we make of this? Bloesch appears himself to be of a divided mind on this mutuality. On the one hand, we are to hear out the warnings of the

26. For this and others, see Bloesch, *Christian Foundations,* pp. 158-60.

27. As in Bloesch, *Christian Foundations,* pp. 166-67 and *passim.* See also Gabriel Fackre in *What About Those Who Have Never Heard?: Three Views of the Destiny of the Unevangelized,* ed. John Sanders (Downers Grove, Ill.: InterVarsity Press, 1995), pp. 71-95 and *passim.*

28. Quoted by Bloesch, *Christian Foundations,* p. 170.

29. Bloesch, *Christian Foundations,* p. 164.

Reformers about invoking the saints, yet, on the other, perspicacity does not prevent us from learning from Archbishop Temple to ask the saints "to pray for us." But the route is not direct, for we "may request their aid in our prayers to God and Christ."[30]

Bloesch's efforts to make good on the third thesis of interrelationship are not as convincing as the first two. The Phillips-Lewis communication is at cross-purposes with his wise words about the dangers of "spirit communication." So too the right attention to the Reformers' warnings alongside the request for the saints' prayers, albeit made circuitously through "God and Christ." The Reformation's word to believers to trust "Christ alone" is here at stake. Bloesch seeks to honor that by routing requests to the saints through the one Savior. While this is a right christocentric instinct, it tacitly assumes that Christ needs assistance in his saving work, the suspect "and" that the Reformers were flagging in their *solas* on ultimate authority. Surely Christ can choose to use both angels and saints in his mission and ministry, but that is his decision to make, not ours to direct.[31] The history of the "cult of the saints" as deflecting from hearing the "one Word" and worship of the one Lord bears out the Reformers' warnings.[32]

In sum, an outstanding evangelical theologian reminds forgetful evangelicals and inattentive ecumenicals of the fullness of the Body of Christ, its heavenly as well as earthly dimensions. And more, of the import of that bonding in mutual remembrance and intercession. The *koinonia* of the church is a life together that transcends time as well as space.

Alternatives in Ecclesiology

Among the alternatives to the ecclesiology developed in this volume there is one that is having its effect on the present state of the church, notably in

30. Bloesch, *Christian Foundations,* p. 165.

31. On the ministry of angels vis-à-vis the work of Christ, see the author's "Angels Heard and Demons Seen," in *Theology Today* 51 (October 1994): 345-58.

32. In a footnote, Bloesch cites the writer's admonition to pray *with* the saints as an example of a view that counsels us to "pray with the saints who have gone to glory rather than for the saints and them for us." As indicated above, the writer holds that we can and should pray for the saints, even as they pray for us. My point was, as here, that we pray *with* the saints and not *to* the saints. See Gabriel Fackre "Jesus Christ in Bloesch's Theology" in *Evangelical Theology in Transition,* ed. Elmer Colyer (Downers Grove, Ill.: InterVarsity Press, 1999), p. 113.

the conversion of important thinkers and not a few others from mainline/
oldline and evangelical Protestantism to the Roman Catholic Church and
to Eastern Orthodoxy.[33] It is illustrated by two writers who have done sub-
stantial work on the doctrine of the church, R. R. Reno and Reinhard
Hütter. The former analyzed the present state of primarily western Protestantism in his work, *In the Ruins of the Church*, arguing that critics should
stay in residence and there make a witness. Later, in an apologia, "Out of
the Ruins," he announced his conversion from the Episcopal Church in the
United States to the Roman Catholic Church.[34] Reinhard Hütter in the
volume *Bound to Be Free*,[35] an updated version of his earlier, *Suffering Divine Things*,[36] made a powerful case for a third way of dealing with the
Protestant disarray in the three topics in his sub-heading — ecclesiology,
ethics, ecumenism (invaded as they are by the "modern daydream" and the
"postmodern nightmare") — one seeking to avoid the false options of either liberal "subjectivism" or fundamentalist "objectivism." In 2004 Hütter
converted from the Evangelical Lutheran Church in America to the Roman
Catholic Church.

With a retrospective eye, it is possible to see the trajectory of the author
toward Rome in *Bound to Be Free*, though that decision was foresworn in
this book as proximate to the "objectivism" there critiqued. Hütter's bril-
liant analysis of the state of the church and prescription in his pre-
conversion period gives us a good clue as to why his "third" way may indeed
lead instead to the second way taken in the recent spate of conversions. And
it provides us here with an alternative to this volume's ecclesiology that
clarifies the options for those troubled by the present state of the church.

Hütter's principal contention in *Bound to Be Free* is that the being of
the church depends on the Holy Spirit's establishing of "core practices"
and "binding doctrine":

> What is most crucial is that faith's "form" cannot be isolated either
> from the church's core practices or from doctrine, since such an at-
> tempt would be to abstract Christ's presence in the believer from the

33. For some evangelical reflection on this subject, see Mark Noll and Carolyn Nystrom,
Is the Reformation Over? (Grand Rapids: Baker, 2005).
34. R. R. Reno, "Out of the Ruins," *First Things* 150 (February 2005): 11-16.
35. Reinhard Hütter, *Bound to Be Free*.
36. Reinhard Hütter, *Suffering Divine Things: Theology as Church Practice*, English translation (Grand Rapids: Eerdmans, 2000).

Spirit's work, from the Spirit's means of conveying and enacting this qualification that *is* the gospel proclaimed and taught. Christ's saving presence cannot be separated from the Spirit's sanctifying mission as enacted through his particular work. This is why doctrine needs to be carefully distinguished from the gospel yet it cannot be separated from it, because the latter is secured through the specification of the former. In other words, doctrine is another form of enactment of the gospel in analogy to the church's core practices — yet under a different aspect: doctrine's *pathos*, its own qualification through the gospel, is constituted by the binding formulations of the gospel's proclamation and teaching in the context of its internal challenge, distortion or rejection. Doctrine is thus completely qualified by the gospel in committing itself in a binding way to a distinct teaching and by distinctively rejecting a particular teaching or set of teachings. Thus the saving knowledge of God, the gospel proclaimed and taught, is mediated and specified by both the church's core practices and by doctrine.[37]

In this illuminating statement, we find a Chalcedonian "distinction without separation" accent applied to the relation of gospel to doctrine, except that, unlike the relation of the divine nature to the human nature in Christology, the gospel depends on the doctrine for its survival in the church, even as the former funds the latter. Indeed, inseparable from the latter as "binding" must be the church's power to reject false teaching as well as to articulate true teaching.

Associated with the importance of binding doctrine for the being of the church are the "core practices." In another key passage, Hütter raises a question about the adequacy of Word and sacrament as the defining characteristics of such (as in the *satis est* of the Augsburg Confession, Article 7, earlier noted, which asserts that "it is enough" to have the pure preaching of the gospel and the right administration of the sacraments to have "church") by citing Luther's "more mature ecclesiology" with a much more extensive list of "core practices":

> In the third part of his treatise, *On the Councils and the Church*, probably the best summary of his mature ecclesiology, Luther develops a much richer and denser account of the relationship between the

---

37. Hütter, *Suffering Divine Things*, p. 51.

Holy Spirit and the church than we tend to find in the standard Protestantism of "word and sacrament." As I set forth in chapter 2, Luther identifies a set of particular practices as the church's constitutive marks. In them we encounter not only "church" but also the Spirit's concrete work, through which he fulfills his own sanctifying mission in the triune economy of salvation. These constitutive marks, or core practices, include the proclamation of God's word and its reception in faith, confession and deed; baptism; the Lord's Supper; the office of the keys, or church discipline; ordained ministry; prayer, doxology, catechesis; and the way of the cross or discipleship. . . . For Luther, these practices not only identify the church but *make* it "church" in the strict sense. That is why I tend to call them "core" practices.[38]

Core practices thus transition from Word and Sacrament to the above longer list, a move of significant import.[39]

At first sight, the stress on binding doctrine and core practices appears to be very much a Lutheran move in the *finitum capax infiniti* tradition.[40] Christ is "haveable" in the church, as the early Bonhoeffer expressed it, questioning Barth's stress on the divine sovereignty and with it the Reformed temptation to press the distance of Christ inordinately from the givens with their Zwinglian tendencies in the sacraments or Barth's "actualism" in ecclesiology.[41] However, when the core practices are detailed as Hütter does, and the binding includes the importance of rejecting authoritatively false doctrine, one must ask where this kind of "church" exists. Given the indictment of mainline Protestantism, and indeed Hütter's own acknowledgment in *Bound to Be Free* of the persuasiveness of convert Erik Peterson's critique of Barth (though in this book not with Peterson's "constructive turn"),[42] it is not hard to conclude that Rome and its magisterium fit the specifications of the core practices cited and the demands of

38. Hütter, *Suffering Divine Things*, p. 50.

39. It is interesting that the volume of essays based on a conference produced by the Center for Catholic and Evangelical Theology (of which the writer is a board member), *Marks of the Body of Christ*, ed. Carl E. Braaten and Robert W. Jenson (Grand Rapids: Eerdmans, 1999), is structured according to this later list of core practices by Luther.

40. See the writer's commentary on this difference in perspective in Gabriel Fackre and Michael Root, *Affirmations and Admonitions* (Grand Rapids: Eerdmans, 1998), pp. 1-43.

41. Dietrich Bonhoeffer, *Act and Being* (Minneapolis: Augsburg Fortress Press, 1996), pp. 90-91.

42. Hütter, *Bound to Be Free*, p. 235 n. 27.

binding doctrine with the authority and readiness to reject false teaching. Such is an alternative to the ecclesiology of this volume. In our idiom, it concludes that, beginning with a similar diagnosis of the state of the church, the way ahead is a return to the historic steward of unity, sanctity, catholicity, and apostolicity, one requiring a tactually successive apostolic ministry with its papal head.

The latter trust in the securing of the attributes of the church by an apostolic ministry raises sharply the question of polity. The validity of "church" appears to stand or fall by this power of guardianship so necessary as a core practice for the maintenance of binding doctrine. This is clearly an alternative to a feature of the polity that is premised in the first paragraph of this section. That is: the church exists as the assembly of believers in which the gospel is proclaimed and the sacraments are celebrated faithfully. Whatever else is added for the well-being of that assembly — the covenanting of faithful congregations, their presbyteral, episcopal, or even apostolic and papal ordering — the rudiments of ecclesial life are in the assembly of Word, Bath, and Meal, *kerygma* and *leitourgia,* apostolicity and catholicity, adumbrated in the models of herald and sacrament. Where that is found, Christ's Body is alive. Whether well, also, that is another matter.

Are we back at sixteenth-century issues? Perhaps. Yet, in our twenty-first-century setting, it entails dealing with a proposal that we can be rescued from the erosion of the gospel by a return to Rome, rather than flight from it. But such a proposal must face the sixteenth-century question about Rome itself. Is there evidence that the faith is actually guarded by the historic episcopacy?

Before answering that about Rome (or Constantinople), let us begin with the Anglican stewardship of historic episcopacy, though such is yet to be fully acknowledged by Rome or Constantinople. The Anglican communion at the beginning of this century is in a struggle for its own continued worldwide existence, as large sections of its constituency believe that its own episcopal order has not secured its classical faith, but, in fact, has undercut it. Further, the fracture of this communion is yet further evidence of the failure of episcopacy to secure a community of "binding doctrine."

But what of Roman polity? Has it secured that church against the acids of modernity and postmodernity? A charitable judgment of the stewardship of doctrine by the hierarchy of that church from Vatican II forward will acknowledge its faithful witness on major questions that have confronted all Christians during this period — defending Christian particularity yet with an openness to larger truth where it can be found; principled stands on war and peace, life and death, however Christians might disagree on aspects of them or the prioritizing of issues; fresh initiatives to other Christian bodies and a will to ecumenical outreach; and more.

Granting the fidelity of official declarations on core doctrine, do these function as "binding" within the Roman Catholic Church? Binding in the sense of alternative perspectives and their proponents disciplined by the power of the keys, as required by Hütter's list of core practices? Given the widespread deviance from stated norms of papal and episcopal teaching by both well-known teachers of that church, numerous priests, some of its bishops, and many of its laity, it is difficult to make a case for the securing of Roman Catholic doctrine by Roman Catholic ministerial practice.[43] The election of Cardinal Ratzinger, the leading figure in guarding the purity of Roman Catholic faith, as the next pope, Benedict XVI, is itself evidence of that church's recognition of the less-than-binding nature of its doctrine on its own constituency. Time will tell of his predictable effort to make it so.

We cross a line from doctrine to "life" when turning to the pedophile and ephebophile scandals in this church. Yes, the Donatist position that grace is tied to moral qualifications in those who preside at the eucharist must be rejected. However, while grace still abounds through the ministries of "the whiskey priest" (Graham Greene), it is also true that behavior is a teaching moment. As such, the fact that significant deviance from the moral-cum-doctrinal norms of Roman Catholicism could go on among the priestly teachers for so long, and is yet to be fully acknowledged and repaired by that church, is commentary on how well this ordering of ministry secures the *kerygma*.

Finally, we return to a profound observation on these matters that comes from a cardinal within the Roman Catholic Church, the one who is its ecumenical officer and whose ideas were earlier cited. Indeed, Hütter quotes these words himself, suggesting a path other than the one he himself later took:

43. Monthly columns of Richard Neuhaus in the journal *First Things* challenging this deviance is tacit admission of its spread. An example of the sharp internal disputes is the critique of leading American Catholic figures including Neuhaus, George Weigel, Michael Novak, and Joseph Fessio by Garry Wills in "Fringe Government," *New York Review of Books,* October 6, 2005, pp. 46-50.

Identity is a dialogical reality, and ecumenical dialogue is therefore dialogue in truth and love. Therefore ecumenism is no one-way street, but a reciprocal learning process, or — as stated in the ecumenical encyclical *Ut unum sint* — an exchange of gifts.[44]

To say that ecumenism is not a "one-way street," means in this volume that the solution of doctrinal disarray is not found in walking the road to Rome. As much as the counter-evidence just cited is the fact that there are stretches of the universal Christian community that show signs of the Spirit that are less visible in the Roman Catholic Church, and thus are needed by that church to be more fully one, holy, catholic, and apostolic. And vice versa. Thus, part of the polity issue here raised has to do with being on the ecumenical path toward a church yet to be in its well-being and also in its *full* being.

Luther's list is important, as Hütter has pointed out. But it needs a more careful sifting and sorting than Luther, the "irregular theologian," has given to it, or as interpreted by Hütter in the subsequent solution to the disarray he finds in mainline Protestantism.

More specifically, returning to the dialogue with Miroslav Volf, while the fundaments of "church" can be found in the assembly of believers with the marks of the church, that particular congregation is inseparable from a historical stream that has flowed from the first century to its present manifestations through a conduit, however cracked and leaking. Such an assembly, as a congregation — or as a denomination — is not its own creation but is dependent for its existence on the church universal over time. Having the apostolic and catholic attributes as they appeared in like manner in the *kerygma* and *leitourgia* of the first Christian community, they are creatures of the Holy Spirit, have promise of all the signs of that Spirit, and thus enjoy the *esse* of church. Yet, and here the list of the later Luther is germane in touching its diaconal accents, as in its willingness to suffer and in the discipline, for the *bene esse* of that church — congregation or denomination. Without a visible sign of subjective holiness — *diakonia* — the church is one of ill-being, not well-being; sick, and at worst, sick unto death.

To the *esse* and *bene esse* of the church must be added its *plene esse.* To be *fully* what it is called to be, no congregation or denomination can live a

---

44. Hütter, *Bound to Be Free,* p. 15.

life apart. Life Together is who God is and what God intends for the church (John 17:21). That means communion with the church longitudinal and latitudinal, ecumenism in both the length and breadth of the church universal. There is no church that now has a lock on this door; no denomination — whatever its formal claims — *is* that church universal. It is only one organ in the full Body of Christ, needing the other parts of the Body to be whole. Until the *eschaton* the church is afflicted with a Corinthian hauteur, and must listen ever and again to the Pauline Word: "The eye cannot say to the hand, 'I have no need of you'" (1 Cor. 12:21). So again Luther's list that comprises, for example, issues of ordained ministry and how it can best be exercised, including as argued above, a historical ordering associated with the historical conduit of the Spirit's work, whatever the church's failures to keep it in good repair. Such an ordering does not supply *the* corrective to the parlous state of much of the mainline Protestant churches. The signs are still present in the "Temple of the Spirit" to be found among the ruins, indeed aspects kerygmatic, liturgical, diaconal, and unitive from which the Roman Catholic Church, in its interpretation of "one, holy, catholic and apostolic" — a church not without its own ruins — can learn for both its well-being and full being on the path toward unity.

A path from where? For those of us in the mainline Protestant churches in the West, the path is from "the ruins" in which we presently live. That place brings with it a Reformation gift, as crucial today as it was in the sixteenth century: the church exists where the Word is preached and the sacraments are celebrated faithfully, where the Spirit's visible works of *kerygma*/apostolicity and *leitourgia*/catholicity are manifest and thus the Spirit's invisible gifts of *koinonia* and *diakonia,* with their attendant hope, promise, and mandate of visibility. Will denominations die and the churches reconfigure in terms of a life together of those faithful assemblies? Or will a new church rise from within the ruins? We shall see what the Holy Spirit has in store for us. For now, pastors are called to go about their witness to and in a community of finite and fallen sinners called to be the Body of Christ. As always, this Body will be marked by the faithful proclamation of the Word and celebration of the sacraments, promised the signs of the Holy Spirit in the mission to bring the world to know and participate in the Story of God through its *kerygma, leitourgia, diakonia,* and *koinonia,* and accorded thereby the attributes of apostolicity, catholicity, sanctity, and unity.

Conclusion

W hy should a busy pastor enter this demanding conversation on the doctrine of the church? This volume presumes that they have something to contribute to that dialogue as they struggle in an actual congregation, firsthand, to discern the signs of the times and search for signs of the Spirit. And as this book is written to aid them in their ministry, it also presupposes that they have something to learn from the long grapple of the larger church to see and search out the same signs.[1]

Close up, that congregation looks a lot like the larger church when viewed through the lens here used: a diverse people showing the variety of signs delineated. Here a company of *koinonia,* there a company of *diakonia,* here a company of *kerygma,* there a company of *leitourgia.* Argued throughout this work is that these are to what the technical terms of unity, sanctity, apostolicity, and catholicity refer. Where these attributes are to be found, there is the church. And for those in the Reformation tradition — so much depends on two of them, the marks of proclaimed

---

1. Hence the importance of partnership between pastors with congregations and the educational institutions of the church with the opportunity afforded thereby for mutual learning. The same things should also be true in terms of give-and-take among pastors and academic theologians in the setting where the pastors do their work and witness. The writer has benefited from forty-five years of participation in Theological Tabletalk groups of pastors and teachers, a model for this kind of mutual fructification.

Word and worship-centered sacrament. And who is called to steward these latter mysteries? There is so much at stake here for pastors and why they need to be in this conversation, both to speak and to listen.

What does the pastor do with this doctrine? For one, a pastor in exercising the "royal office" helps to build up the Body of Christ, strengthening the members that represent one or another of these charisms of the Holy Spirit. For another, in that same role, the pastor helps each part see that it needs the other organs for the Body to be healthy and whole. For another, the pastor in the same office helps the congregation discern and deepen the signs of the Spirit within the denomination of which that congregation is a part. For another, the pastor in that same office enables the congregation to discern the signs of the Spirit wherever they may be found in the church universal, strengthening the ties that bind Christians who manifest those signs. In all these aspects of the pastoral calling, the pastor is led by the vision of the church in the fullness of its being, its *plene esse*.

Conjoined to the royal ministry are the prophetic and priestly offices, the stewardship of Word and worship. Custodianship of these marks of the church, assuring that they faithfully come to be in whatever form that may take — in the intimacies of the small group or the public praise and prayer of a cathedral — are by the work of the Holy Spirit the way Christ keeps the Body alive, even as the stewardship of those offices of the laity keeps it alert and moving in the world.

In Chapter 1, the signs of the Spirit were discerned as fiery tongues that swept down from above, then from inside the community out to the world. In Chapter 2, account was taken of how these same signs appeared in pastoral purview over the decades. In order to feel the pulse of the times, signal manifestations of *kerygma, leitourgia, diakonia,* and *koinonia* were traced with the Acts 2–4 distinctions of inreach and outreach, nurture and mission more implicit than explicit. In this conclusion, a simple schematic is offered to suggest how the four signs, which we have argued correspond to the classical attributes and are related to the Reformation marks and the more contemporary classification of models of the church, actually can and do appear in the life of a congregation. The chart below has been tested over the years in conferences and congregations, and appears in the writer's and

2. *The Christian Story,* vol. 1, *A Narrative Interpretation of Basic Christian Doctrine,* 3rd edition (Grand Rapids: Eerdmans, 1996), p. 167; Dorothy and Gabriel Fackre, *Christian Basics: A Primer for Pilgrims* (Grand Rapids: Eerdmans, 6th printing, 2000), p. 82.

spouse's earlier texts for both pastors and laity in one form or another.[2] It provides a framework for a pastor and congregation to measure their life against the model of the Acts community, and thus constitutes an incentive for a fuller witness in this one place to the apostolicity, catholicity, holiness, and unity of the church universal. Further, the compartmentalization of the signs, in their inward and outward expression, are a local expression of the divisions that characterize the church at large. Any move toward the fullness of the church local has its counterpart in the church at large, the chart being a guide for the honoring of the "models of the church" found there and a guide and incentive in the quest for a church truly ecumenical.

The central column is the "nature" of the church as it has been identified here as manifest in the four signs of the Holy Spirit. In the column on the left are the manifestations of those signs within the life of the community — the inreach of the Spirit of Acts 2. The parallel column on the right represents the outward movement of each sign as described in Acts 3–4. In each case the descriptions attempt to connect with usage in this volume and current language.

SIGNS OF THE SPIRIT

Inreach — Nurture		*Outreach* — Mission
getting the Story straight preaching and teaching	*kerygma*	getting the Story out evangelism
celebrating the Story within sacramental worship	*leitourgia*	celebrating the story without public prayer and praise
doing the deed within service to the brothers and sisters in Christ	*diakonia*	doing the deed without service to the world as victim-care and victim-cause
unity within the Body of Christ	*koinonia*	unity within the body of the world

The Church Universal in the Grand Narrative

"The church" — a chapter in the Story that moves from creation, through fall to covenant to its center, Christ, then to the Body of Christ on earth, and from there through salvation to consummation. Without the pentecostal people, there is no knowledge of this narrative. An apostolic community is the bearer of the apostolic teaching. And into the hands of this Body is given the Book in which we hear the Word. Some in this company are called to be special tellers of the Tale.

Pointers to the church to be are to be found all along the path of the Story. Its ecclesial life together is anticipated in the Life Together of the Persons of the triune God out of whose being and purpose rises the drama. In creation's chapter 1 the will for the world is the same one-ness enjoined upon the Body of Christ. In the fall of the world in chapter 2 is the resistance that continues in the brokenness of the Body. In chapter 3's Noachic covenant with the world is the Spirit's rainbow sign that will stretch yet further over a future Temple. And in the covenant that makes its way into the world of Abraham and Sarah, a people of God is brought to be in continuity with one to come. At the center of the Story — chapter 4, the story of Jesus Christ within the encompassing Story — the long-sought reconciliation is won! In chapter 5 the church is born in acts of telling, celebrating, doing, and being. To the Word that so goes forth comes the graced response of justifying faith busy in the sanctifying love of chapter 6. And the final chapter, the fulfillment of the divine purposes, the life together of God and the world, has no more need for a sign of Things to Come, for "I saw no temple in the city, for its temple is the Lord God the Almighty and the Lamb" (Rev. 21:22). Until those latter days, the church is among us as temple, body, and people to witness to the Lamb. This is the Story the pastor is called to tell and celebrate.

Dare we hope for a new birth of the mainline churches? Is a fresh Pentecost possible for us? Where the signs of the Spirit are to be found among the signs of the times, the answer is "Yes." In that lies our hope.

Index

Index